MISTRIAL
OF THE
CENTURY

MISTRIAL
OF THE
CENTURY

A Private Diary
of the Jury System on Trial

TRACY KENNEDY
and JUDITH KENNEDY
with ALAN ABRAHAMSON

Judith Spreckels, *Trial Historian*

DOVE
BOOKS

ISBN 0-7871-0687-9

Printed in the United States of America

Dove Books
301 North Cañon Drive
Beverly Hills, CA 90210

Distributed by Penguin USA

Text design Stanley S. Drate/Folio Graphics Co., Inc.
Jacket design by Rick Penn-Kraus
Cover illustration by Bill Robles
Tracy Kennedy and Judith Kennedy photos by Rick Penn-Kraus

First Printing: August 1995

10 9 8 7 6 5 4 3 2 1

Tracy is the calmest, most easy-going person I have ever met. He is very comfortable with who he is. He is methodical in his reasoning and is always eager to learn.

Judy is who she is today because of Tracy. As she sees it, she was an old, old woman when they met. She thought old, looked old, acted old. Tracy taught her that always living in the future can age a person. He taught her to live one day at a time: "stop and smell the roses" so that she then would have "selective memories" for today!

They have a unique relationship. The kind women and men dream of and one that novelists write about.

They have an **unconditional** love. There are three kinds of love in the Greek language. **Philos**—brotherly love; **Eros**—erotic love; and **Agape**—Gods' kind of love. Not, I love you if . . . ; or I love you because . . . ; or I love you when . . . ; I love you "anyhow." They feel they have all three kinds of love, especially **Agape.**

To Tracy's mom and dad, to Judy's mom, Nellie;
to our sons William and Thomas
who demonstrated an Agape kind of love,
loving us "anyway" through our silence
and never asking questions.

—T.K. and J.K.

❧

To Laura and Kayla
—A.A.

Acknowledgments

Special thanks to Amtrak for allowing their employees to participate in Jury Duty without financial duress.

To our collaborator, Alan Abrahamson, who had the knowledge of an attorney, the insight of a pilot, the mind of a journalist and the heart and wisdom of Solomon. Our special thanks for helping us put our words and feelings on paper.

To our friend and attorney, Michael Kassan, COO, Western International Media Corp. for encouraging us to put our experience into words and for introducing us to Arthur Barens.

Special thanks to Michael Viner and his lovely wife Deborah Raffin, who realized this was uncharted territory and urged us to take a stand by writing this book.

To Attorney William Bennet Turner for his encouragement and valiant attempt to persuade the judge to return my handwritten personal diary.

To Dr. Raymond Manning who is as close as the phone and never too busy to listen. He will always be remembered.

ACKNOWLEDGMENTS

To Dr. Bruce Weimer, our friend and physician, who always knows the right thing to say. His encouragement to tell our story and not to keep Memorial Day a secret really promoted this book.

To Dennis Holt, President, CEO, Western International Media Corp. for his support of this project.

To Kathleen Stringham who could always tell when we needed a hug.

Very special thanks to Theresa Cisneros, Weletta Kirk, Michelle Dyck, Susan Fowler, Reddy Chada, Jackie Awalt, Carol Gambrel, Rich Percival, Margie Robinson, Barbara Robertson, Curt Borman, Joyce Bergstrom, Ron Gaertner, Steve Van Trees, Lee Bullock and Judge Richard M. Bilby, United States District Court, District of Arizona, Tucson.

To Avi Cohen, Producer, CBS News, who has become a close friend. He has been such a help to us in so many ways. He knew about Memorial Day weekend but chose to allow us to tell our story in our own time. We will always be grateful to him.

To Ann Cole, President of Ann Cole Opinion Research and Analysis, who befriended us and invited us to sit on a panel at the American Society of Trial Consultants Convention.

—T.K. and J.K.

✦

My editors at the *Los Angeles Times* graciously allowed me to pursue this project. Thanks to all of them. I also want to salute each of the *Times* reporters covering the Simpson case; their spectacular work made my research that much easier.

ACKNOWLEDGMENTS

Everyone at Dove was thoroughly supportive. Michael Viner offered me this opportunity, which I truly appreciate. Mary Aarons saw it through from start to finish. Lee Montgomery was a delight. So was Jacquie Melnick. I am particularly grateful to Judith Spreckels for her advice and hard work.

Tracy and Judy Kennedy showed real courage by confiding in me and trusting me enough to work with them.

Thanks to Phil Hager, Phil Carrizosa and Marc Katz for teaching me about journalism.

At home, Pearl Hicks was, as always, a wonder. So was my mother-in-law, Judy Hudson, who volunteered for extra babysitting duty.

My mother, Sandra Abrahamson, also joined the babysitting parade. But I appreciate and love my mom for so much more. Her support for me—as it has been for each of her four sons—has never wavered.

I would also like to thank Bob and Patti Rosichan for their unqualified love and support over the years.

Finally, there is my beautiful and loving blond bride, Laura. Thank you for everything—for believing in me and, most of all, for sweet Kayla Anne.

—A.A.

Contents

Preface   *xiii*

1   Scales of Justice   *1*

2   A Desperate Soul   *4*

3   Awfully Depressed   *10*

4   Make Me a Promise   *15*

5   With Every Wish . . .   *18*

6   Welcome to the Justice System   *26*

7   Selected   *43*

8   Rules   *48*

9   Sequestered   *56*

10   Left Behind   *72*

11   Who's Who on the Jury   *80*

12   Culture of Paranoia   *93*

CONTENTS

13   Trial Chronology   *105*

14   In Court   *111*

15   Human Touch   *118*

16   A Bad Honeymoon   *122*

17   Family Visits   *128*

18   Trial Chronology   *134*

19   On Trial   *139*

20   Map People   *148*

21   Investigation   *156*

22   Feeling the Pressure   *163*

23   Trial Chronology   *172*

24   Photos and a Field Trip   *186*

25   Trial Chronology   *197*

26   Disputes and Confrontations   *209*

27   Trial Chronology   *233*

28   Summoned   *251*

29   Excused   *268*

30   Pandemonium   *276*

31   A Kiss Good-bye   *279*

32   Intensive Care   *284*

33   Taking a Stand   *297*

    Aftermath   *300*

Preface

⊤

Tracy and Judy Kennedy are ordinary folks who got caught up in the O.J. Simpson saga. Their lives will never be the same.

When Nicole Brown Simpson and Ron Goldman were killed on June 12, 1994, it had little impact on Tracy and Judy Kennedy. They live in Glendale, California, many miles and several tangled freeways from Brentwood, the upscale community where the bodies were found. In no way did the Kennedys ever expect their lives would ever become so intertwined with what quickly became the most notorious murder case of our time.

By chance, Tracy Kennedy was called to jury duty. He survived round after round of jury selection and, in November 1994, was selected to serve on the jury charged with rendering judgment on O.J. Simpson.

In January 1995, the jury was sequestered. All potential jurors had been living under a news blackout for months and, once sequestered, they were further isolated from the world around them. In addition, their identities were stripped, their names replaced with numbers. They were expected to adhere to strict routine. They constantly found themselves under surveillance—and not just by the Los Angeles County sheriff's deputies assigned to watch them, but, it turns out, even by Superior Court Judge Lance A. Ito.

All in the name of rendering a service to one's community.

To protect the jury from corrupting influence, contact between the jurors and their families was limited. Visits were marked by yet more rules and regulations. The burden on Judy Kennedy—as it was on the families of each and every juror—also proved severe.

Tracy Kennedy was dismissed from jury service on March 17, 1995. It can fairly be said that he barely survived it.

ALAN ABRAHAMSON
August, 1995

MISTRIAL
OF THE
CENTURY

1

❀

Scales of Justice

Tracy

August 1, 1995

Since I was dismissed from the jury, I've had so many people ask me: is O.J. Simpson guilty of murder?

To be perfectly honest, at the very beginning, I thought it improbable if not impossible. How could he have done such a terrible thing, especially to his ex-wife, to the mother of his two children—to a fellow human being?

As I listened to the evidence from Seat Number 3 in the most famous jury box in America, a different thought dawned on me: Violence is a pattern with

O.J. Simpson. It was a part of his life with his ex-wife, Nicole Brown Simpson. He hit her, bruised her, bloodied her. What kind of a man does that to a woman? And what does it tell you about his character and his capacity for evil?

In fairness, we haven't heard all the evidence yet, and it would be wrong to make a final judgment. I have not done so; I would not do so.

It will be with sadness and regret that I learn of a final verdict. I wanted so very much to be a part of that verdict, to have been called to civic duty and to have fulfilled my obligation with pride in a job well done.

Who can tell, however, whether this trial will actually produce a verdict or, instead, the unsatisfactory emptiness of a mistrial? The Mistrial of the Century. Who ever thought such a result was imaginable?

Not me. Then again, I could not have foreseen the incredible public fascination with the case. It is nothing less than obsession. The trial has become a symbol of the American justice system, the benchmark against which all things legal are measured and compared.

That gives me pause. For, in a sense, I wonder if the case is destined to go down in the books as a mistrial regardless of the ultimate outcome in the courtroom—that is, as a miscarriage of justice, a perversion of the jury system, the bedrock on which our system is based.

When the case began, I never could have imagined that events would transpire as they did in the courtroom or behind the closed doors of the jury room.

From the beginning, it was if we in the jury were also on trial—with the system testing our ability to cope under the extreme conditions of long sequestration.

For me, this case has shaken my faith in the criminal justice system. I used to have enormous faith in that system, used to think it was where truth prevailed, where good and able men and women convened to render judgment as the conscience of the community.

Now, I confess, the criminal justice system scares me. I know only too well what it can become if those good and able people are not treated with the respect and dignity they deserve.

2

A Desperate Soul

Judy

May 26, 1995

It was a Friday night, the start of the long Memorial Day weekend when we ambled down to the Jacuzzi in the courtyard of our condominium complex. Tracy lowered himself into the water and settled into a corner. He stared off into space. For a while, he didn't say a word. Then he announced that he had decided to kill himself.

I sat there, stunned and silent. What to do? What to say?

I tried to think fast. It was hard to make sense of

it all—of all that he could be feeling and everything
that had happened since he was dismissed as a juror.

The bubbling water in the Jacuzzi had always been
a soothing tonic for both of us. It was a wonderful
part of our routine. A Jacuzzi is almost a California
cliché, I know, but it was where we could relax at the
end of a long day, feel the bubbles and the heat, and
enjoy each other's company. It had always worked its
magic on both of us. But not since Tracy had been
dismissed from the O.J. Simpson jury. Ten weeks had
passed, and still he was not right. He was not the
calm, positive Tracy I knew.

For the past few days I had noticed that he was
distant, staring into the water or off into space. He
was present physically, but not mentally. We weren't
connecting, and that was so unusual as to be almost
unreal. We are best friends and have always connected. So during this period, I asked him several
times, "Anything bothering you?"

He'd answer, "No, nothing I can't handle."

"Well, why don't you talk to me about whatever it
is? You'll feel better. Maybe if you talk it out, maybe
that's what you need."

"No." He kept saying he'd just have to handle it.
"Everything will be OK," he said.

But over the last several weeks, he had become
quieter and quieter. He'd also been complaining that
he hadn't been able to sleep, so I had suggested a
visit to Bruce Weimer, a neurologist in Pasadena.
Bruce is a friend of ours as well as an M.D., and he'd
done wonders for me. I suffer from migraines, and

he had prescribed medication as a part of migraine therapy that helped, so I felt confident about suggesting that Tracy go see him. "Talk to him," I had told Tracy. "Tell him how you're feeling."

Tracy had seen Dr. Weimer earlier in the afternoon, and when he came home, he had a prescription for an antidepressant. Tracy is not the kind of person who believed in depression, certainly not in the medical or clinical sense of that word. It's not in his vocabulary. If you're down, you snap out of it. He had no patience with people who said, "I'm depressed." He'd say, "Look, just get busy. Do something. Do whatever." Depression, he felt, was a real weakness. So he simply took the prescription and didn't fill it. When he came into the house, he was carrying the prescription in one hand and, in the other, a notice from the County of Los Angeles, the official gray-and-pink notification form for jury service. He'd been excused from service on the O.J. Simpson jury two months earlier and, of all things, now he was hit with another one of these forms.

As he came through the door, the look on his face was one of complete hopelessness. There was such a resignation about him. His shoulders were drooping. He looked like a very old man, tired of life.

That night in the Jacuzzi, he seemed so lost. We live in a rambling condo complex in Glendale, northeast of downtown Los Angeles, and though the complex is busy, with the pool and Jacuzzi usually the center of attention, we had the Jacuzzi all to ourselves. It was a soft, warm spring evening; the stars twinkled in the sky above as we dipped our toes in the bubbles below.

After some time, I took a deep breath and braved a question: "What are you thinking about?"

"We've got to talk," he replied.

"OK," I said, feeling a distinct sense of alarm.

"You've got to promise me," he said, "that what I'm going to tell you, you won't tell anybody."

"OK."

"Promise me also that you'll forgive me."

"OK," I said again and thought, what could this be? Why would he need to ask for forgiveness?

I had been sitting on the steps of the Jacuzzi, holding on to the handrail. As Tracy gripped the sides of the spa with his hands, alternately fixing, then releasing, his grip against the concrete railing, I slid into the water to be close to him. The light built into the Jacuzzi floor was powerful and threw off a shocking brightness at night. It shone straight up, illuminating Tracy's chin but throwing the rest of his face into an eerie darkness. In the blackness, his face masked in shadow, he began to speak.

Tracy talked at length about how difficult it had been for him to go back to work since he had been dismissed from the jury. He couldn't concentrate. He felt that others were looking at him and whispering behind his back, nudging each other and saying, "There's the one, that's him, the one who got thrown off the O.J. jury." He felt the dismissal marked him as a failure. Judge Ito had excused him for what Tracy later found out was "abundant good cause," according to the judge. Tracy had been devastated.

Though some time had passed, he still couldn't concentrate. He said he'd looked into retirement, but if he was to retire now, at fifty-three, he would get none of his Amtrak pension. He had examined his finances and he just wanted to quit it all, leave everything behind. "I just have to get away," he said.

I thought he was saying, "Let's separate." You know, "I need to get away. Get things sorted out. I don't want to have to worry about finances and whatever." I was thinking he wanted to leave me and this was his way of telling me.

So I said, "Well, would you feel better if you packed your things and just went off on a trip for a while?"

"No," he said. "That's not what I'm thinking."

"Do you want a permanent separation?" I still was not getting it.

"Well, sort of."

He began to talk some more, saying he couldn't handle it anymore, had to get away, really just had to get away. "Now don't try to talk me out of it," he said. "I've made up my mind. I've thought through everything. I even have the time worked out."

This was Friday. On Tuesday, after the long weekend, Tracy was supposed to leave for a month-long business trip. So I still didn't realize what he was getting at.

We kept talking. About fifteen minutes later, it hit me. He was saying he did not want to live. He talked some more, then wound up by saying, "I don't want you to feel like it's your fault, that it's anything with you. I want you to forgive me because it's not you.

We have such a special relationship and the way that I'm feeling right now and the way that I can't handle things, I feel our relationship will only go downhill from here. I can't stand the thought of it changing. Yet I can't stand the thought of living without you. And I can't quit my job because we can't afford to live and I would lose my pension, so the only thing I know to do is, I have to kill myself."

I was, as I said, stunned. Finally, I said, "Now you've really thought about this?" It was all I could think of.

"Yes. I've made up my mind."

3

✝

Awfully Depressed

Tracy

May 26, 1995

Dr. Weimer met me in the waiting room at his office. He walked in and looked at me and said, "You know, when I saw you on TV the night you were excused from the jury, you looked to me like you were shell-shocked."

"Well, Doc," I said, "I'm in bad shape." I had tears in my eyes. All I could do was cry, and he knows I'm not a crier.

We slowly made our way back to a room where we could talk. "I need something to help me sleep," I said.

"What are you taking now?" he asked.

"Xanax." Judy had them in the house for her migraines.

"Stay away from Xanax. I don't want you taking any more of those. You're down and you don't need anything to help you stay down. You need something to help you get back up. Antidepressants. You're awfully depressed."

"Well, I haven't been sleeping, and I need something to help me sleep."

"I'm not going to give you anything for sleep. I'm going to write you a prescription for Zoloft. I want you to take three of them a day. That'll help you deal with this thing."

"Well, right now I can't sleep. I need something to help me sleep."

"We'll worry about that when you start getting yourself back together."

He recognized right away that I was in bad shape. I was. But I really didn't know it. And I did not know just how bad off I truly was.

Since I'd been excused from the jury, I'd lost twenty pounds. I'm a runner and that keeps me thin, so that was twenty pounds I couldn't afford to lose. It made me look haggard, weary, beaten. A lot of people at work said, "You're losing an awful lot of weight. Are you trying to?" I would say, "No. I'm not." I resented the question and the intrusion into my privacy. People meant well but I couldn't handle even a simple question like that. I'd come home and I'd be exhausted. I had no appetite. I'd be so tired. I'd try to go to sleep thinking, I have to go to sleep because I have to get up. But I couldn't sleep.

It never occurred to me that I was depressed. To me, depression meant you were simply having a bad day.

But I couldn't shake it. And I kept coming back and back, over and over, to the feelings that had dogged me, nagged me, berated me, hounded me, given me no peace since I had been excused March 17. Failure. I had failed. I was ashamed. I had failed everyone and everything, let down all the people who had been depending on me. Who had I failed? The better question was, who hadn't I failed? I had let my fellow jurors down. I had let Judge Ito down by not continuing to do the job I had been drafted to do. I had let down the prosecution and defense. I had let down the families of the victims by not finishing the job. I had let Mr. Simpson down by not participating fully in giving him a fair trial. I had let down the state of California as well as the entire nation because the process of a fair trial is one of the pillars this country is based on, the way that ordinary citizens can partake in the justice system, in freedom itself.

How had it gone so wrong? I was excited to be picked for the jury. More than that, though, I felt almost a patriotic calling to serve—to fulfill the responsibility of being a juror, of being the most important link in the justice system with honor and pride. The fact that this was America's most famous celebrity murder case made it more challenging. The question of O.J. Simpson's guilt or innocence had captured the nation. The issue raged in bars, barber shops, bowling alleys and even at work. It dominated TV, radio, newspapers, and magazines ever since the infamous low-speed chase that led back to the estate and O.J.'s arrest. As jurors, we had a powerful responsibility. O.J. Simpson's future hung in the balance. We knew two people were dead and their families longed for justice. We were mindful of their rage yet had to remain focused on what was just.

I'm no legal expert. Before the case began, I decided not to dwell on it. I paid no mind to the endless parade of talking heads on TV, the nonstop speculation among lawyers, journalists, talk-show hosts, professors, and the self-appointed "experts." The day of the chase? I was watching the National Basketball Association finals on TV. The interruption of the game was exasperating. Still, during the months after the murders, I couldn't help but pick up the basics: no murder weapon, no eyewitnesses, a trail of blood that led from the murder scene to O.J.'s white Bronco and into his house. The evidence was all circumstantial. It would be up to the prosecution to prove motive, means, and opportunity.

Like the others in the group of twenty-four originally picked for the jury, I came prepared. But it didn't take long for the experience to sour. We were private citizens asked to give up everything that meant anything—our jobs, regular contact with our families—for the benefit of the system. In turn, that system turned on us, locked us up in a routine that was regimented and impersonal, a mix between boot camp and prison. Most of Los Angeles County sheriff's deputies assigned to take care of us acted as if they were guards and we their prisoners.

After many months of tension, all my thoughts and feelings were finally coming together. I was able to piece together in my mind the threads, the wisps of emotions that had been preying on me for ten weeks. I could finally articulate it all in my mind, realize that's what it was, and I couldn't deal with it.

When I came home from the doctor's office that Friday afternoon, prescription in hand, I noticed the gray-and-pink form in the mail. I looked at it and it really hit me hard. A form from the county? Was I available for jury service? This was the exact same thing that I'd gotten when this whole thing started. And I said to myself, "Oh, no. No, no, no. They're trying to get enough people together to have another trial if this thing goes into deadlock or they lose enough jurors where they can't complete it." Not the most rational line of thinking, not terribly lucid, I know, but that's what I was thinking. And I thought, oh, no, not again.

4

Make Me a Promise

Judy

May 26–27, 1995

Not only had Tracy made up his mind to commit suicide, but he intended to talk about it just this once, while we were in the Jacuzzi, and that would be it. "After we talk about it tonight," he said, "I don't want to talk about it anymore."

I was thinking, OK, Tracy had the prescription, but it had not yet been filled. It usually takes about three weeks for the medicine to do its stuff.

"Make me a promise," I said to Tracy.

"What?"

"Make me a promise that you will at least take this medicine for a month. Then go back and see the doctor. If you're still feeling like this, then let's have the same conversation again."

I was still trying to think furiously. I was already planning ahead. On Monday morning I could get back to work, I could call the doctor, I could say something, I could tell him it's serious. Oops! Monday was a holiday. I could do all this on Tuesday. Was it worth calling Dr. Weimer at home? Did I still even have his home number lying around somewhere? Where could I have put that phone number? No. Wait. Be calm. Just how serious was this? Was this a cry for attention or the real thing? If it was the real thing, what was the right thing to do? Call the suicide hotline? Or was that an overreaction? Think! But stay calm, appear assured, don't panic.

Tracy and I talked for a long time that night. He said he had done some checking. There were certain bank accounts in his name, and he had already written checks out to me to put into a different bank account. He talked about things like this and I sat there calmly and told him, "Yes, I'll forgive you and I know it's not about us, it's this trial, but is there anything I can do?"

After about two or three hours of talking, Tracy promised me that he would wait a month. He would take the antidepressants, see the doctor, and then, if we needed to, we would talk again. And finally we went to sleep.

❡

The next morning, it was as if nothing had happened. Of course, Tracy had said the night before, "Once we have this conversation, we've had it. Once it's over, it's over." And it was over. But it was as if it had never really occurred.

He seemed sort of himself again. We went to the grocery store and shopped for the holiday. We were going to grill. That afternoon we watched a movie and made love. Saturday was a perfect day.

That night we went out to the Jacuzzi again, but this time it was just like it was supposed to be. We enjoyed the night air, the peace of floating in the water. We came back into the condo and got ready for bed and he said, "Now, what I want you to do is to make sure you put your laundry out in the laundry basket because I'll get up early Sunday morning and do the laundry so you can sleep in."

As I drifted off, my world once again seemed settled. I would not have to worry. We would get through this together. Tracy leaned over and kissed me good night. It was a tender kiss full of love and sweetness.

In fact, he was kissing me good-bye.

5

With Every Wish . . .

Judy

In certain ways, this fix I found myself in was partly my own doing. I had been excited about Tracy working on the Simpson jury. I kept pushing him forward, urging him to be excited about the process, because I thought it would be a life-changing experience. Little did I know how terribly prophetic that would prove to be.

I had been on juries myself and had found the experience rewarding. Also, I know my husband, and I believe the system needs people like him.

Tracy is one of those people who has the ability to

look at a problem, take it apart, examine it from all directions, get different perspectives, and piece it back together. He also is the kind of person who demands information before making a decision; he doesn't make snap judgments. I knew that he would listen carefully to the evidence and take it apart. I knew he would listen attentively to what other jurors had to say, and when he came to a decision, he would stand by it. This is the kind of decision making the system needs.

When Tracy is convinced about something, he stays there. He disagrees with people's ideas, but not the people themselves. He is a straight shooter. He tells you exactly what he thinks. People don't need to worry about where they stand because he lets them know, unequivocally. For some, this quality can be intimidating. He asks questions and demands answers. For those who are insecure, he may appear as a smart-aleck. But I know the truth. He is both a gentleman and a gentle man.

He's not necessarily a leader. He's a very private person and enjoys being by himself. Because he's such a loner, I assumed sequestration would not be a burden. He's always thought of himself as the kind of person who gets lost in the shuffle, who falls through the cracks, who gets overlooked. But he's self-reliant and that has made him confident in his judgments. No matter what goes wrong, no matter what I do, he has an uncanny ability to reassure me. He simply looks at me and smiles with this little glimmer in his eyes. "The only thing that is earth-shaking is death and taxes," he says. "Those are the only things you have to worry about in life, so just calm down, it's going to be OK." No matter what was going on, I could always pick up the phone and say to him, "Just talk to me," and as he did, I'd lose myself in his soothing, calm voice.

Never, ever, has Tracy had an ego that needs to be fed. Actually, we both have gone through that time in our lives when it seemed important to be someone, to obsess about prestige. That's in the past. We don't need others around to tell us that we're OK.

All these qualities, I felt, would be valuable if he was selected for the Simpson jury. I used to say to him, "If you get to do this, it will mean a lot to the system." I thought the system would be lucky to have him.

I know I'm lucky to have him. We met when we were both living in New Orleans. We had gotten there by very different routes. He's originally from Florida, attended Ohio State University, did a hitch in the Air Force, worked for Bell Labs, then for Amtrak in Jacksonville, Florida, signing on as an electrician. He knew a great deal about airplanes—he even had a commercial pilot's license—but didn't know the first thing about trains. After a while, he was promoted to technical trainer and moved to New Orleans. I'm from North Carolina and lived most of my life in the South. I graduated from the University of Southern Mississippi with a degree in music education. I then taught school for twenty years. For many of those years I had a tremendous weight problem. I was grossly overweight; at one point, I weighed 210 pounds. One day I realized that the weight had to come off. So I became interested in behavior modification and in dieting. I did master's work in psychology and lost almost a hundred pounds. At the time, music education was being eased out of the schools, so I moved to New Orleans and got a real estate license. One day, a man called the office where I was working and said he wanted to look at some homes. He said he was single and he liked things that were removed from the fast pace. He liked being by himself and wanted enough house so that he had room to move around in. I knew exactly which house was the right one; it was one I had picked out for myself. So I took him to see several other houses and then to see this one. And it was just a real click. He loved it.

I felt a real click with Tracy, too. It wasn't just that he got along so well with my two young sons, I also could really talk with him. I was going through a divorce and he had been down the same road. Neither one of us wanted to be involved with anyone ever again. So there was no pressure when we talked, just a feeling of safety. We felt comfortable with each other and soon became good friends.

And yet, as we got to know each other, it turned out there was more to it than a feeling of safety. There was electricity and a passionate excitement. We were very, very close friends but over a period of two years there developed this wonderful chemistry, a certain magic, between us. We could communicate with our eyes. Without saying a word, we could communicate volumes. We still can. I realized there was something behind his eyes that was so much deeper than what he allowed other people to see. Those eyes were intriguing, beguiling, entrancing. To this day I find myself lured by his eyes, drawn to them, enchanted by them.

Neither one of us wanted to be married again, but as the saying goes, never say never. Several years later, we were married. On our wedding day, I felt I had married the most wonderful man in the entire world. And now, eight years later, I can still say that. He's my best friend. We still love to be playful around each other, remind each other how much we treasure the other. We even have a little code we use when one of us is traveling. Whoever is on the road will call the other at home and let the phone ring once. Just once. If I'm out of town and the phone rings just once at home, Tracy knows that it's me calling to say "I love you."

We moved to California because Amtrak transferred Tracy out to the Bay Area. I didn't particularly want to move, because in real estate you need to know people, need to know the place you work in, and I wouldn't have that out west. For Tracy, it was definitely a step up, a supervisor's job with an emphasis on teaching others various Amtrak systems. I had to scour the want ads, looking for something different. I saw in the ads that Jenny Craig was hiring. Given my background and my interest in psychology, the position seemed ideal. I was at Jenny Craig two months before I was promoted, then was promoted again shortly after to the corporate human resources department. And then, within a year, Tracy was transferred again, down to Los Angeles.

I resisted the move to L.A. I thought everyone in

L.A. was twenty-five, blond, and hard-bodied and wore thong bikinis to work. I just didn't want to be in that atmosphere. We had just gotten settled in the Bay Area and, more importantly, had emotional ties there.

Tracy had literally just arrived in San Francisco on the night of the big earthquake in October 1989. When they asked for volunteers at his hotel, he went willingly out into the night, searching homes about four blocks from the section of freeway that had collapsed near downtown Oakland. Both he and I felt a sense of place in the Bay Area, a sense that we belonged there. Plus, he loved his job as an instructor. He enjoyed the process of teaching, particularly when he would explain something in a class and would see the light of understanding pass across a student's face.

His job, however, beckoned. So we moved to Glendale, a dozen miles northeast of downtown Los Angeles. This was a very deliberate choice, one that reveals certain qualities of Tracy's personality. He bought several maps that showed, from a pilot's point of view, the air flow in and around Los Angeles. We wanted a place where the air drove the smog somewhere else. On the maps, that was Glendale, so we bought a condo and settled in. I got a new job working for Western International Media, the nation's largest media management company, leading seminars in stress management and sensitivity training, fields of particular interest to me. So life, even in Los Angeles, turned out to be most pleasant for nearly four years until the arrival of the summons for jury duty in the summer of 1994.

When it arrived, there was no indication that Tracy would one day find himself in the midst of the Trial of the Century. In fact, initially he was directed to report to a courthouse where juries hear civil cases, not criminal trials. Odds were he'd hear some dispute involving a fender bender or some dry and boring contract hassle.

I hoped Tracy would actually make it to a jury. I had told him several times how lucky I felt to have served as a juror. In truth, though, that's probably because I was fortunate enough to have been ordered (during one of my two jury stints) to the courtroom of Judge Miriam Waltzer, the first woman elected to serve on the criminal court in New Orleans.

It was a child abuse case in which prosecutors had charged the parents with criminal neglect and were seeking jail time. I don't remember much about the particulars, not even the ultimate outcome, but I do remember the way Judge Waltzer handled the courtroom. Not only was she sensitive, she was in complete control. You knew that everything would be handled correctly and graciously.

If anyone in the courtroom said anything during jury selection that was derogatory, even about the police, she would tell people they didn't realize what a wonderful system we had and how much respect they should have for it. Her demeanor was so compelling that she made you feel glad to be in America.

When it came time for the two children to testify, Judge Waltzer stopped everything and said, "Now, I want to tell the attorneys: You may not raise your voice. You may not point your finger. You may not use three-syllable words. And we're going to bring these children in one at a time." They brought in a little girl first, and Judge Waltzer took off her robe. She got a piece of peppermint and walked over near the witness box, where she sat down on the floor next to the girl and said to her, "Tell me what your name is." The little girl did. "Do you know what telling a lie is?" the judge asked. The little girl said yes, and so the two of them talked. And that's the way she swore in the little girl. Then, the whole time the child testified, Judge Waltzer sat there close to her. It was incredibly moving. Not once did the little girl look at her mother. After the child finished testifying, Judge Waltzer said, "The court wants to take this witness to get ice cream."

A little boy testified next and Judge Waltzer treated him the same way. I was so impressed with the sensitivity she exhibited when dealing with these children. It was mesmerizing.

Last summer, when Tracy's jury summons arrived, I thought of Judge Waltzer. I wanted Tracy to be a part of this, to see for himself how the court system works.

How does that old saying go? With every wish . . . there comes a curse.

6

☥

Welcome to the Justice System

Tracy

September—November 1994

I viewed jury duty as a civic responsibility similar to being drafted into the armed services to fight for your country. That's what I thought when I received my jury summons. I'd been drafted to do a civic duty.

Besides that, I was interested in the law, how it was carried out. It would be a good experience, Judy told me. She said I would learn things. She promised it would be interesting.

O.J. Simpson was arrested June 17, about five days after his ex-wife, Nicole Brown Simpson, and her friend Ron Goldman were found dead. My summons demanded my presence on September 13, 1994, at a building in Los Angeles called Civil Courts West. It never crossed my mind that I could possibly end up on the Simpson case.

That first day was a cattle call. There were 300 people there. They quickly cut our group in half and ordered me back two weeks later.

This second time the count was about 200. They had added more people and then cut us in half again and ordered us back in two more weeks.

On October 12, I was back again. It was then that it dawned on me that this was for the Simpson case. The process of jury selection was also a frightening introduction to what lay ahead.

I always carry a Swiss Army knife. It's one of the fancier models, a couple inches long, with a few gizmos and a black case. We hadn't been told not to bring any pocketknives, but at the door of the Criminal Courts Building I was informed in a brusque manner, "You can't bring that in here." "What am I supposed to do with it?" I asked. "I don't care," the guard said. "You're not bringing it in here." Of course, there was a long line to get through the metal detector. The detector was so sensitive that a few women had to take off their earrings and others had to take off their glasses. I had finally made it to the front of this line and I couldn't get in unless I ditched my knife. I didn't argue. I left the line and asked for a volunteer to hold it for me. What else was I going to do? A bunch of TV camerapeople had gathered near the door and one of them volunteered to hold the knife. "I have a knife just like that," he said, adding that he was almost sure to be around the courthouse until the evening.

Upstairs, the crowd had grown to 300 prospects again. After a while, Mr. Simpson, Judge Ito, and the lawyers came in the room. It was the first time I'd ever seen O.J. Simpson in person and I thought, wow, this is really it. There were a lot of oohs and aahs from all the prospective jurors in the room. Here they all were: Mr. Simpson and his incredible smile; Mr. Shapiro, complete with the look of a skillful, powerful lawyer; and Mr. Cochran, who exudes confidence. Looking at Ms. Clark, I knew she was a very capable person. The same with Mr. Hodgman—solid. It was impressive to see all the famous names, in person, big as life.

I still couldn't believe it was possible I'd be selected. And I couldn't fathom the possibility that O.J. Simpson had actually committed the crime for which he was charged. Truly, it seemed impossible.

The selection process then began in earnest. We were each given an enormous questionnaire to fill out: 79 pages, 28 parts, 294 questions. Judge Ito had announced to all of us that he had cut it from 500 questions. This, I thought, is going to take a while. There were a lot of grunts and groans from the people around me; apparently they thought it was an intrusive pain, too. Or maybe, like me, they were annoyed that we didn't have anything to write on; you had to fill out this big thing on your knee.

It took me four full hours to fill out the questionnaire, and I worked quickly. I didn't elaborate. I put down the truth and assumed they must have had good reasons for asking these questions:

No. 1: Age.

No. 2: Are you male or female?

No. 3: What is your race? White/Caucasian, Black/African-American, Hispanic/Latino, Asian/Pacific Islander, Other.

No. 4: Marital status: single and never married, single but living with nonmarital mate (for how long?), currently married (length of marriage), divorced (when divorced, length of previous marriage, did you initiate the divorce—yes or no), widowed (length of marriage).

No. 14: Where were you born?

No. 15: Where were you raised?

No. 19: Are you currently employed outside the home? Yes or no. If so, by whom are you employed? Full- or part-time? If part-time, how many hours per week? How long have you been so employed?

No. 29: Do you have any close friends or relatives who either have worked or are currently working in journalism or in the news industry in any capacity? Yes or no. If yes, please state where and when s/he was so employed and give a brief description of his or her duties.

No. 82: The witnesses below testified at the preliminary hearing. Please check the witnesses you recall and describe your impression of each:

Allen Wattenberg (owner of knife store)
Jose Camacho (knife store salesman)
John De Bello (restaurant manager)

MISTRIAL OF THE CENTURY

Karen Crawford (restaurant bar manager)
Stewart Tanner (waiter)
Pablo Fenjves (neighbor)
Steven Schwab (dog owner and neighbor)
Sukru Boztepe (neighbor)
Bettina Rasmussen (neighbor, Sukru Boztepe's wife)
Allan Park (limousine driver)
Brian "Kato" Kaelin
Rachel Ferrara (Kato's friend)
Los Angeles Police Department (L.A.P.D.) Detective Philip Vannatter

No. 86: Please describe your impressions concerning the lawyers for O.J. Simpson:

Robert Shapiro
Johnnie Cochran
Gerald Uelmen
Alan Dershowitz
Robert Kardashian
F. Lee Bailey

No. 87: Please describe your impressions concerning the lawyers for the people of the State of California:

Marcia Clark
William Hodgman

No. 93: If you have discussed this case with friends and/or relatives, do your friends/relatives overall seem to lean toward thinking that O.J. Simpson is: not guilty, probably not guilty, not sure, probably guilty, guilty.

No. 94: This case will be closely followed by local, state, national, and international electronic and print media. What is your reaction to this?

No. 95: On average, how often have you talked with relatives or friends about this case? Answers range from "never" to "5 to 10 times a day."

No. 101: Did you call the police, the judge, or either the defense or prosecution "800" hotline number regarding this case? Yes or no. If yes, please explain.

No. 113: Have you ever had occasion to regularly drive through the Brentwood area? Yes or no. If yes, please explain the circumstances.

No. 114: Have you visited the location of 875 S. Bundy since the date of the killings of Nicole Brown Simpson and Ronald Goldman? Yes or no. If yes, how many times have you gone there? Please describe your reason(s) for going there.

No. 132: Have you ever met O.J. Simpson? Yes or no. If yes, please explain the circumstances.

No. 144: Have you ever written to a celebrity? Yes or no. If yes, whom did you write?

No. 156: Have you purchased or otherwise obtained any commercial item relating to this case? (For example: a T-shirt, book, video, or trading card.) Yes or no.

No. 170: When is violence an appropriate response to domestic trouble?

No. 176: What do you think is the main cause of domestic violence?

No. 182: How big a problem do you think racial discrimination against African-Americans is in Southern California? A very serious problem, a somewhat serious problem, not too serious, not at all too serious, or not a problem.

No. 185: How would you feel if a close family member or relative married someone of a different race? Would favor it, would not oppose it, would oppose it. Please explain.

No. 197: Have you followed any of the court hearings concerning DNA analysis in the Simpson case? Yes or no. If yes, please check all the media sources that apply. (From a list of ten TV stations, including Court TV; four newspapers; three radio stations; five magazines; and five "tabloids," including the *National Enquirer*.)

No. 204: Did you vote in the June 1994 primary elections?

No. 211: Have you ever provided a urine sample to be analyzed for any purpose? If yes, did you feel comfortable with the accuracy of the results?

No. 212: Do you believe it is immoral or wrong to do an amniocentesis to determine whether a fetus has a genetic defect? Yes, no, or don't have an opinion. Please explain.

No. 222: Do you have (please check) security bars, guard dog, alarms, weapons for self-protection?

No. 244: What type of books do you prefer? (For example: nonfiction, historical, romance, espionage, mystery.)

No. 254: What accomplishments in your life are you most proud of?

No. 274: Name the most significant sports figure, sport program, or sporting event scandals you recall.

No. 275: Does playing sports build an individual's

character? Yes or no. Please explain your answer whether you answer yes or no.

No. 276: Do you seek out positions of leadership? (please check answer) Always, often, seldom, or never.

No. 277: Please name the three public figures you admire most.

No. 284: How do you feel about being a juror in this case? Please explain.

No. 293: Is there any matter not covered by this questionnaire that you think the attorneys or Court might want to know about you when considering you as a juror in this case?

It's hard to believe there could be anything not covered by that questionnaire. I still don't understand why they wanted to know some of the things they wanted to know.

While we were filling out the questionnaire, one comment came up over and over again: "This is so personal." You could hear it muttered all about the room.

"Your responses on the questionnaire will eliminate having to ask these questions in open court," the instructions to the form said. We were told that if a question seemed too personal, we were to write "too personal" on the form. On my very last page I put something like, "I'm a very private person. I don't want to be public." I'm not used to giving out personal information and I was apprehensive about doing so. I have a thing about not letting Big Brother get into my mind or my business. Even well into the process, I wasn't fully certain what it was I was getting into, so I wrote a letter to the judge:

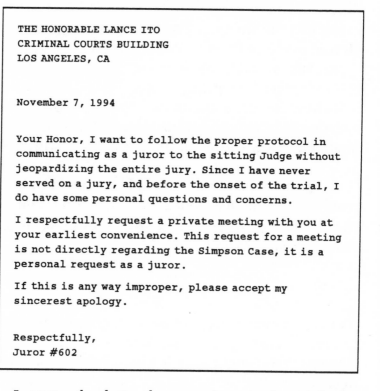

```
THE HONORABLE LANCE ITO
CRIMINAL COURTS BUILDING
LOS ANGELES, CA


November 7, 1994


Your Honor, I want to follow the proper protocol in
communicating as a juror to the sitting Judge without
jeopardizing the entire jury. Since I have never
served on a jury, and before the onset of the trial, I
do have some personal questions and concerns.

I respectfully request a private meeting with you at
your earliest convenience. This request for a meeting
is not directly regarding the Simpson Case, it is a
personal request as a juror.

If this is any way improper, please accept my
sincerest apology.


Respectfully,
Juror #602
```

I wrote the letter because I wanted to ask the judge, first of all, how I could go about speaking with him if I had any questions. I had no idea. More importantly, I wanted to make sure we were indeed going to remain anonymous and I wanted to know about sequestration and possible conjugal visits.

Eleven days went by. Deirdre Robertson, Judge Ito's clerk, an incredibly pleasant woman, took me aside on November 18 and said that any request to the judge had to be in writing.

My primary concern was that we remain anonymous. The judge, lawyers, and clerks seemed to be striking a bargain with us. If we would offer our services as jurors, in return, no one in the public or press would ever know our names or where we worked.

That didn't happen.

No one used my name in open court. I acquired an identification badge and a new name: Juror 602. But when we came back to the courthouse in early November for one-on-one questioning with the attorneys, Mr. Cochran asked me if I worked for Amtrak. I was under oath; I had to say yes. But it was in open court. And I hadn't yet told my boss at work that I was in the Simpson jury pool. That's the way I wanted it. If selected, my intent was to serve, then go back to my normal life, without any publicity. He also asked what I did for Amtrak in the training department.

I was so disturbed by Mr. Cochran's question that I wrote a letter to the judge. (See page 36.)

After that, I got a copy of my questionnaire. But I was told that *voir dire*—that's the formal name for the jury selection process—was generally conducted in open court and that any other notes that related to me, if there were any, would not be available to me, the public, or the press until the trial was over. Now everyone knows what happened with this. Everyone at work knew from the beginning I was part of the Simpson jury because of information supplied about jurors in various newspapers.

THE HONORABLE JUDGE LANCE ITO
CRIMINAL COURTS BUILDING
LOS ANGELES, CA.

NOVEMBER 19,1994

Dear Judge Ito:

On November 7, 1994, I requested a private meeting with you at your earliest convenience.

Friday, November 18, 1994, Deirdre called me and asked that I put into writing my request to you.

In the first meeting of the prospective jurors and alternates, we were promised anonymity. I have been told by people at work that my description and the place of employment that was disclosed on television, radio and in print, makes it obvious that I am one of the jurors.

Therefore, I would respectfully request that the questionnaires, transcripts of my <u>Voir Dire</u>, notes from the Prosecution and the Defense be sealed, if possible at this time, and returned to me at the conclusion of the trial.

I would respectfully request that I be given a copy of anything pertinent to me, (at the time of the release) to the media, the law students observing the proceedings, or anyone else.

If this is in anyway improper, please accept my sincerest apology.

Respectfully,
Juror #602

✦

The selection process was a grind; at best, tedious, at worst, painfully slow and consistently boring. We kept losing people, some excused by the court when they said they couldn't serve on a sequestered jury, others who complained of economic hardship and said their companies wouldn't pay their salaries during jury duty. As I survived each step, I began to think I might actually be selected. After court one day, I went home and told Judy I thought I would be picked. She was very excited. She believed the experience would be great. That day had been long and at that particular moment, I was not all that charged up, but she got me going again.

The long, drawn-out process continued, and my turn finally came to answer questions. Aside from the question from Mr. Cochran about Amtrak, I mostly remember questions from Mr. Shapiro. He went through my questionnaire and asked questions from the answers I'd given on the form. It also seemed like he was trying his case as he was asking me questions, trying to advance the theory that Mr. Simpson couldn't possibly be a killer. Good lawyers try to do that, I know that now, but at the time it seemed a bit odd to hear him asking such elaborate questions that obviously were not aimed at getting information from me, but rather were intended to remind all the potential jurors of the defense's position in the case.

A couple of the responses I'd put on the questionnaire apparently proved interesting. I said that I'd experienced domestic violence in my family when I saw my father strike my mother. I described myself repeatedly as a loner. My wife, I said, had told me I was one of the fairest men she knew. I also said that O.J. Simpson "is kind of a hero of mine." That was really true. I grew up on the wrong side of the tracks. I had read somewhere that O.J. had, too. I used to live in a public housing project. I'd been told that he had, too. I felt those connections keenly and, at one point, when O.J. Simpson was at the height of his football career, I had identified in some small way with him. Except, of course, he was a hell of a football player and I wasn't.

The thing that really seemed to catch everyone's attention in the courtroom, however, was a question that I had for Judge Ito. Was this jury going to have conjugal visits? I did not want to be cooped up for months at a time with no opportunity for intimacy with my wife. Mr. Cochran, perhaps sensing the opportunity for a light moment, asked me how often I would desire such a visit: Once a month? Once a week? More frequently? "Once a day would be nice," I said, and there were laughs in the courtroom.

And just like that, after waiting an interminable time to take my seat in the box, suddenly the questioning was over.

❖

With plenty of time to kill there in the courthouse throughout the months of the selection process, I began to ponder the prospect of a long trial. Especially the notion of sequestration. Once, while listening to a potential juror answer questions during *voir dire*, I found myself thinking, I hope I'm not sequestered with that particular person. I couldn't even tell you why I thought that then, but I remember thinking it.

Frankly, I didn't even know what sequestration really meant. I knew the definition of the word—to separate or isolate—but I didn't know just how separated or isolated the jurors were going to be. When questioned, I even told Judge Ito in open court, "Whatever sequestration means, I'm not really looking forward to that."

I knew the principle behind the idea of sequestration: protecting jurors from outside influences. The case needed to be decided on the basis of the evidence, not what was reported in the newspapers or on TV. I understood that. The potential jurors had already promised Judge Ito that we would not watch anything on TV about the case or read the papers, and I was sticking to that promise. I believe all the potential jurors did. I've never had any reason to think otherwise.

At the beginning, we were led to believe that the case would take about three months. Judy and I talked and we agreed I could do anything for three months, including stand on my head. We planned on handling it the way we handled everything else. We both travel a lot for business and this was just one of those things that comes along. Judy travels for business several times a year, and sometimes I'm gone a month at a time. You take things day by day, go in, do your job, and put up with whatever you have to put up with. But, even early on, I should have been more attuned to the way the deputies were treating us.

From the beginning, it was demeaning.

A few weeks into the selection process, we were waiting in line to get into the building. It was raining, and I had a cold and a sore throat, so Judy had given me lozenges, which I packed in a little ditty bag I always carried for my lunch, along with something to snack on. One of the metal detectors broke down. No one explained a thing. No one cared how long the line was. No one cared if it was raining or cold outside. You just waited to get in. Then, once you were in, you had to go to the ninth floor, where Judge Ito's courtroom is located. As you stepped off the elevators, which were interminably slow, you had to go through another metal detector. On one occasion, I'd actually gotten to the courthouse early and made it to the ninth floor with only one other person in line. The deputies took a look at me and my ditty bag, and I overheard them talking to each other: "What's he carrying there? Is that a purse? What's going on with him?" I put my bag on a conveyor belt and a female deputy said to me, "The machine's broken. We're going to have to search you." The deputy dumped my entire bag out on a table and made a big show of going through everything. Of course, I had nothing improper in the bag. She gave me the all-clear, but then I had to pick everything up that she had dumped out and put it back in the bag while all the deputies watched, none of them lifting a hand or offering to help. After I packed up my bag and sat down, a few minutes later I noticed that the machine had suddenly started working. It wasn't broken at all. I walked back. "Excuse me," I said. "Was the machine not working before or was it just not turned on?" "It wasn't turned on," one of the deputies said, "but you can go through it now if you want to." "No, thanks," I said.

I wanted to let them know that I knew they had lied to me when they told me the machine was busted. This wasn't a very big thing, grant you; it was a little lie. But it was indicative of an attitude. Little lies build up, and it seemed to me that deputies would frequently mislead prospective jurors.

In November there came the moment I hardly expected. Twelve of us were seated in the jury box and asked to stand and raise our right hands.

I was in shock. I could hardly grasp the idea that I'd been selected for duty on the jury. I was numb, literally numb.

And yet, the moment itself seemed strangely anticlimactic. Maybe it's because the selection process was so long and drawn out.

The enormity of it all hadn't hit me, really, until I was on the way home. I thought, wow, I'm on the Simpson jury. My next thought was, *how in the world can I get off?* I felt apprehensive and fearful in addition to a whole range of emotions. It was a call to duty. I figured I had to get through it, like my six years in the Air Force, do myself proud, do a good

MISTRIAL OF THE CENTURY

job. So I wanted to do it. But then I didn't want to do it at all, not even a little bit. This, I thought, is going to be a burden. Although I hadn't kept up with the news and had avoided all discussion of the Simpson case, it was impossible not to know that O.J. fever was in the air and I understood emphatically that this was going to be a devastating responsibility. No matter what decision the jury ultimately made, a lot of people were going to say it was the *wrong* decision.

Panic gripped me and I thought again that I didn't want to do it anymore. I thought, how in the world do I get out of this?

7

⌖

Selected

Judy

November 1994

The night Tracy came home after being sworn in for the jury, I looked at his face and I felt distinct unease.

I couldn't read his eyes. I couldn't tell what was going on inside his mind. I thought perhaps he had been kicked off the panel. I'd already heard on the radio that jurors had been sworn in that day, and yet he looked bewildered, not excited.

He blurted out that he had, in fact, been chosen. You have moments in your life when the enormity of something really hits. You take a deep breath, your

42

eyes open wide, you feel a rush inside, and a weight settles on your shoulders. This was one such moment. We both were sobered by the realization of what was at stake and how serious this was. Tracy was going to be judging a man's life. Two people were dead and their families were demanding answers. There was the press, forever inquisitive. Would we ever again have any peace in our lives?

To cope, I had to push aside these concerns. They were too big. To ask these questions, questions without answers, was futile. I focused instead on the stuff of day-to-day life. That, at least, I felt I could control.

"We need to make plans," I told Tracy.

"Absolutely," he said.

We decided that despite the intense media attention focused on all things Simpson, we wanted to remain as anonymous as possible.

We did not tell our families that Tracy had been selected.

I told my boss and her immediate supervisor and Tracy told his boss.

No one in our condo complex knew.

We rented a post office box and changed the addresses on our bills to that box.

We changed our phone listing to my maiden name.

We felt it was of the utmost importance to stay anonymous. We wanted to keep it as quiet as we could and wanted nobody to know because it really wasn't anyone's business. Our hope was that we would fade back into the woodwork once the trial had concluded, and I certainly did not want to be bothered while it was going on.

If others knew that Tracy had been picked, both of us felt, it would have meant that anyone and everyone would want to talk to us about it. We just wanted to go on about our lives.

So this was the choice that we made. It was a good choice because it enabled us to feel that we had taken control of our lives and a situation over which, in truth, we had very little control. It was also a bad choice because as events unfolded over the next few months, it left me without anyone I could talk to.

The thought of sequestration gave us both reason for concern. But, in truth, it seemed that we already were semisequestered. By November, when Tracy was sworn in, we had been obeying Judge Ito's orders not to read anything about the case in the newspapers or watch anything about it on TV. Tracy was not allowed to wake up to a clock radio. He could not listen in the car to a traffic report.

We both proceeded on the assumption that the trial would last three, maybe four months. I'm independent; so is he. I'm used to doing things, taking care of things when they come along. Had I been a dependent person, a clinging spouse, I could see where a long separation like that could present a challenge. But I reasoned to myself, OK, this will be a separation. A bit on the long side, but still, nothing that's insurmountable. Take it one day at a time. It will be like eating an apple, one bite at a time.

Tracy was fairly adamant about making certain

that we made no mistakes. "When I'm sequestered," he told me, "I don't want you keeping up with the case at all because I don't want you to inadvertently say anything that might have any bearing on what I think or what I'm supposed to be doing." He received no quarrel from me. Plus, the reality was I had far too much to do at work to pay close attention to the case. I commute an hour each way to work, and it's not uncommon for me to work a ten-hour day. I was too busy to worry about breaking the rules.

✵

The holidays came and went. We didn't do much, didn't see many friends or relatives, because that would possibly have put us in the position of talking about the Trial of the Century, and we didn't want that. Also, we knew that Tracy was about to go away, and we wanted to spend time with each other.

By the time January rolled around, we had been in semi-isolation for about four months. I was just beginning to realize how profound the isolation would become for us. It wasn't until later that I realized that no one had really done this before. There were no models to pull from, and very few experiences to serve as real-life guidance. The last big case in which the jury was sequestered like this may have been the Manson trial, and that was a generation ago. I wondered if anyone from the legal community had ever asked anyone from the psychological community what happens if we sequester twenty-four people for x number of days or x number of months?

46

What happens when you put people in a situation where they would be isolated, dehumanized, and regimented? To me, it seemed someone would have done some sort of thinking about that, maybe a doctoral thesis or maybe a law review article. For instance, how did the experience of sequestration impact decision-making abilities? Would the jury be too bonded as a unit to disagree? Wasn't the whole point of the system to seek out independent people who could judge the evidence and find the truth? Or did sequestration produce a different outcome? Did the pressure of living together, of sharing close quarters for an extended period of time, make jurors so hypersensitive to each other's faults that there could be no unity on dinner, much less a murder verdict? Perhaps sequestration had no affect on a jury's decision making, but how could that be? If you were around twenty-three other people for months and months, it had to affect people psychologically, didn't it? And what about the others in their lives? How did sequestered jurors relate to the sheriff's deputies in charge of monitoring them? What special training had the deputies taken to relate to the jurors? Certainly, I reassured myself, the deputies had taken some special courses in interpersonal dynamics. They would be supportive, reassuring, and understanding.

I felt confident that the people in authority had the answers. What could there be to worry about?

8

✦

Rules

Tracy

December 1994–January 1995

In September, Judge Ito had laid down the basic ground rules for service as a juror. We each got the order shown on opposite page.

These were the rules that Judy and I had faithfully been obeying. They seemed direct enough. It wasn't terribly hard to figure out what not to watch on TV.

In December, after the twelve original jurors were chosen and immediately after the twelve alternates were chosen, the judge issued a more particular set of rules. (See pages 50–51).

Now, for the next month, before the trial was to

RULES

SUPERIOR COURT OF THE STATE OF CALIFORNIA
IN AND FOR THE COUNTY OF LOS ANGELES

Date: 23 September 1994
Department 103
Hon. Lance A. Ito, Judge
D. Robertson, Deputy Clerk
People v. Orenthal James Simpson
Case #BA097211

COURT ORDER

Each juror and alternate juror selected to serve in this matter is ordered and directed to:

1. Not to read or listen to or watch any accounts or discussions of this case reported by newspapers, television, radio, or any other news media.

2. Not to visit or view the premises or place where the offense or offenses charged were allegedly committed or any premises or place involved in this case unless directed by the court to do so.

3. Not to converse with other jurors or with anyone else upon any subject connected with the trial unless and until permitted to do so by the court.

4. Not to request, accept, agree to accept, or discuss with any person receiving or accepting, any payment or benefit in consideration for supplying any information concerning this trial for a period of 180 days from the return of a verdict or the termination of the case, whichever is earlier.

5. Promptly report to the court any incident within their knowledge involving an attempt by any person improperly to influence any member of the jury.

Dated: _____   _____
                                    Hon. Lance A. Ito

I agree to the above order and understand that if I violate the provisions of this order that I can be ordered to pay a sanction to the court of up to $1,500 for each violation pursuant to Code of Civil Procedure Section 177.5, to reimburse or make payment to the County of Los Angeles for costs caused by a violation pursuant to California Rules of Court, Rule 227, or punished by a fine or imprisonment for contempt pursuant to Code of Civil Procedure Section 1218.

Dated: _____   _____
                                           Juror

SUPERIOR COURT OF THE STATE OF CALIFORNIA
IN AND FOR THE COUNTY OF LOS ANGELES

Date: 12 December 1994
Department 103
Hon. Lance A. Ito, Judge
Deirdre Robertson, Deputy Clerk
People v. Orenthal James Simpson
Case # BA097211

COURT ORDER

During the course of this trial, and until further order of the court, the trial jurors and alternates in this case shall NOT read any newspaper article or other written account including magazines or books or watch any television programs dealing with this case, the defendant or his family, the victims or their families, the attorneys or any other matter concerning this case. The court will distribute to the jurors and alternates the local daily newspaper of their choice, edited to remove any coverage of this case.

Jurors and alternates shall NOT listen to any radio programming. Each juror and alternate may listen to audio tapes and compact discs, including books on tape that do not concern this case. Jurors and alternates who need current weather and traffic information may get this information by dialing (213) 962-3279.

Jurors and alternates shall NOT watch:

1) ANY television news program or news break.

2) ANY television ''tabloid'' program such as *Hard Copy, A Current Affair, Inside Edition, American Journal,* or *Premiere Story.*

3) ANY television talk show such as *Marilu, Leeza, Jenny Jones, Sally Jessy Raphael, Oprah, Donahue, Good Morning America, Today, CBS This Morning, The Montel Williams Show, The Maury Povich Show, Ricki Lake, Rolonda, Rush Limbaugh* and *Geraldo.*

4) <u>ANY</u> television news magazine program such as *60 Minutes, 20/20, Dateline, Eye to Eye, 48 Hours* or *Primetime Live.*

5) <u>ANY</u> entertainment news magazine such as *Entertainment Tonight* and *EXTRA.*

6) CNN, CNN Headline News, CNBC, The E! Channel, *Sports Center* on ESPN, *Press Box* on Prime Ticket, *The News* on MTV, any news or talk show on BET and *Dennis Miller Live* on HBO.

7) *The Tonight Show (Jay Leno)* and *The Late Show with David Letterman.*

Jurors and alternates <u>MAY</u> watch:

1) Normal television entertainment programming, including sports and home shopping channels, not excluded above, <u>however, jurors are strongly cautioned to avoid watching advertisements for upcoming news broadcasts known as</u> ''teasers.''

2) Cable or satellite television channels: American Movie Classics, Showtime, Cinemax, The Disney Channel, The Movie Channel, The Shopping Channel, The Family Channel, The Cartoon Channel, Turner Classic Movies, MTV, Discovery Channel, Arts and Entertainment (A&E), Bravo, Lifetime, Nashville, Nickelodeon and Home Box Office.

3) Movies and other programming on video tape that do not involve this case, the defendant or his family, the victims or their families, or the attorneys and their families.

Any questions regarding this order shall be directed to the Clerk of the Court, Mrs. Deirdre Robertson at (213) 974-5726.

<u>IT IS SO ORDERED.</u>

begin, we were forbidden from listening to *anything* on the radio. The TV was, in theory, still available— but for "National Geographic" specials, "Barney the Dinosaur," "Tom and Jerry" cartoons, and "Brady Bunch" reruns. Fifty-seven channels and nothing, absolutely nothing interesting that we were allowed to watch.

Inherent in these rules was the unavoidable sense that we were being treated as children, not as grown men and women with a diversity of viewpoints who were being asked to bring their common sense to an issue of great public interest and concern. The next list we got from the court (see opposite page), as the day of actual sequestration drew near, served only to heighten that feeling.

This list was a joke. But it wasn't comical. It was as if we were eight-year-olds being packed off to summer camp and the counselors had sent our mommies and daddies a list of do's and don'ts. Personal hygiene items? Only a little bit of cash? And, moms and dads, be sure the campers leave those cameras and radios behind; where they're going, they won't be needing them.

Interestingly, the check-off list made no mention of the most ubiquitous business tool in America—the personal computer. There was no indication whether a portable computer would pass official muster, and I spend hours upon hours with my IBM clone. One of the great things about the machine is that you can play CDs while you use other programs, and I do that frequently. Plus, for Christmas, I had gotten a new chess program for the computer, and I really wanted

RULES

```
        JUROR'S PERSONAL CHECK-OFF LIST

                                                    Check

PERSONAL HYGIENE ITEMS
    Toothbrush/toothpaste                          _____
    Brush/comb                                     _____
    Nail clippers/file                             _____
    Deodorant                                      _____
    Shampoo                                        _____
    Blowdryer                                      _____
    Curling iron/curlers                           _____
    Soap                                           _____
CLOTHING
    Clothing appropriate for court and leisure
    time. Keep in mind that relatives may visit up
    to two times a week and can bring additional
    clothing or items as needed.                   _____
SHOES
    Shoes appropriate for court and light
    recreation (walking, etc.).                    _____
MEDICINE
    Aspirin, prescription medicine, chapstick.     _____
EYEGLASSES, SUNGLASSES                             _____
CASH
    Not an excessive amount. Relatives will be
    allowed to bring additional amounts if
    necessary.                                     _____
FAMILY PHOTOS                                      _____
LETTER WRITING MATERIAL                            _____
WATCH                                              _____
MAKE-UP                                            _____
WALKMAN OR SIMILAR LISTENING DEVICE
    Cassette or CD player only.                    _____
    Listening tapes or CDs.                        _____
BOOKS, PUZZLES, PLAYING CARDS, GAMES               _____
DO NOT BRING
    AM/FM RADIOS
    MAGAZINES OR NEWSPAPERS
    CAMERAS/VIDEO CAMERAS
    EXPENSIVE JEWELRY
    KEYS

NOTE: ALL ITEMS MUST BE CHECKED BEFORE CHECKING INTO
      HOTEL. THIS IS TO ENSURE THAT THE COURT IS
      SEQUESTERING A JURY THAT IS FREE FROM OUTSIDE
      INFLUENCES.
```

to test myself against that chess game. Given the slow pace at which the Simpson case was moving, I figured that there would be abundant downtime for me to play chess. I had no intention of writing a book on the computer, or taking notes for a book on the computer, or anything that would violate my oath as a juror.

Having learned my lesson in November, I knew now that if I wanted something, I had to write the judge a letter:

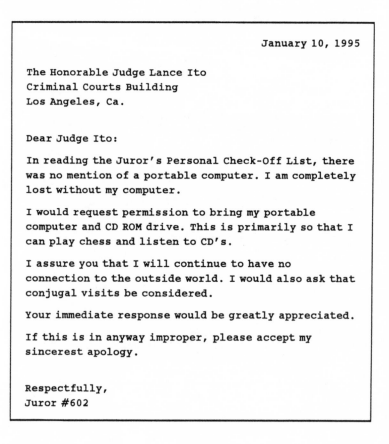

> January 10, 1995
>
> The Honorable Judge Lance Ito
> Criminal Courts Building
> Los Angeles, Ca.
>
> Dear Judge Ito:
>
> In reading the Juror's Personal Check-Off List, there was no mention of a portable computer. I am completely lost without my computer.
>
> I would request permission to bring my portable computer and CD ROM drive. This is primarily so that I can play chess and listen to CD's.
>
> I assure you that I will continue to have no connection to the outside world. I would also ask that conjugal visits be considered.
>
> Your immediate response would be greatly appreciated.
>
> If this is in anyway improper, please accept my sincerest apology.
>
> Respectfully,
> Juror #602

Permission was granted, but I should have known what was coming. I had to sign a formal legal statement saying that I would use the computer only for my chess game and to listen to CDs.

DECLARATION

I, TRACY KENNEDY, do depose and state as follows:

1. I have personal knowledge of all matters set forth herein, and if called as a witness to testify, I could and would competently testify thereto.

2. I am a trial juror on the case of PEOPLE VS. ORENTHAL JAMES SIMPSON.

3. I will use my personal computer for personal uses only.

4. I will not use my personal computer to take notes or to generate any information in the case of PEOPLE VS. ORENTHAL JAMES SIMPSON, CASE NUMBER BA097211.

I declare under penalty of perjury under the laws of the State of California that the above is true and correct.

Executed on _____, 1995 at _____.

_____
TRACY KENNEDY
JUROR NO. 0602

With sequestration upon us, I felt good that I'd be able to use my computer. We still didn't know, though, about those conjugal visits . . .

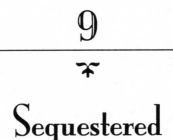

9

Sequestered

Tracy

January 11, 1995

It was a gray and rainy day. It had poured all night and in the morning there was no letup. Everything seemed gloomy.

A few days before, we'd gotten a call from the court clerk. We'd been told to gather at a secret location near Dodger Stadium. Pickup time, as explained on a direction sheet we were also given, was 0900 hours. Nine A.M. sharp. Don't be late.

This was easier said than done, especially given rush-hour traffic in Los Angeles. On any given week-day, the Golden State Freeway, Interstate 5, one of the main north-south arteries through downtown Los Angeles, is jammed solid with traffic. In the rain, drivers in Los Angeles slow down to speeds that people in Chicago or New York would find hilarious if it wasn't so aggravating. In a driving rain, like the one we had that Wednesday morning, traffic inched ahead.

It was raining so hard that we could barely see where we were going. We weren't sure which exit to take; we had only been in the Los Angeles area for about five years and weren't familiar with all the freeways yet. Both Judy and I were wound up and nervous, and the trip to our rendezvous location made us even more tense. We barely spoke a word in the car.

The secret spot was on a side street. Miraculously, we made it there on time. The parking lot was a sea of umbrellas. Underneath all those umbrellas, desperately trying to stay out of the rain, people were milling about and kissing each other. At that point, you couldn't tell who was a juror and who was a family member, since the jurors didn't know one another or the alternates all that well yet. The whole scene was a bit like morning recess on the playground on the first day at school. Or, given the check-off list we'd been given to prepare, the first day at summer camp. You wanted to introduce yourself to everyone, but the process was a bit odd:

"Hi, remember me? I'm Number 602 and this is my wife."

"Oh, hi. Nice to meet you. I'm Number 320. So nice to meet you. And you, too, Mrs. 602."

Herding us about were uniformed, armed sheriff's deputies. I watched some of the passing cars go by and wondered what the drivers thought of the curious scene.

Finally, the deputies took a head count. All twelve jurors and twelve alternates were present and accounted for. The deputies gave us a few minutes to say our farewells, then motioned us toward these white government vans with tinted windows. Within minutes, we'd be off into the rain, and the unknown, twenty-four perfect strangers, ready to meld together, were headed for some hotel—no one knew where—in the capable hands of dedicated public servants, all of us, deputies and jurors alike, committed to a search for truth and justice!

Or maybe not.

Maybe it happens like that in the movies. In real life, and especially given the constraints of an operation run by the government, particularly an agency of county government, things work differently. The operating principle of county government is Murphy's Law: If it can go wrong, it will, and at the worst possible time. In keeping with that principle, there were supposed to be three vans, but one of them was in the shop or somewhere. The deputies couldn't fit all the people and all the bags into the two vans, so they announced they'd have to make a couple of trips.

Some of us dashed for the vans, if only to get out of the rain. I was one of the lucky ones. I found a seat in the first van, and off we went.

As we pulled away from the curb, several people

inside the vans turned and waved. We moved along, and the people left behind got smaller and smaller. After we turned, they were gone. And we were by ourselves, with all our bags and everything, being chaperoned around Los Angeles by armed guards. We were strangers. Alone and yet together. Sequestered. Isolated from everything and everyone except each other.

For a moment, all was quiet. But you could feel a sense of adventure and excitement percolating. Then the comments came fast and furious.

"Where do you think we're going?"

"This hotel had better be OK."

"Do you think the food will be good?"

Everyone was friendly. It was the beginning of a grand and glorious adventure. Together we had embarked on the ride of a lifetime. Cooperation, team spirit, and friendliness seemed to be the order of the day.

After a ride that actually proved quite short, just down a few streets, we arrived at the hotel. We could see out the windshield that it was a first-rate hotel. One more positive thing! Cheers rang out.

The deputies unloaded us in the underground parking garage. We had to wait for the stragglers to arrive. Then, all together, we were directed into the elevators and rode up to the two floors specially reserved for us, the O.J. Simpson jury.

And there, any notion that this was going to be like summer camp evaporated instantaneously. Boot camp and prison are more apt comparisons.

"Line up over here, please," the deputies announced. "It is necessary that we search you and your luggage." The women went to one room, the men to another.

We walked through a metal detector. Then deputies ran an electronic wand over each of us, just like guards do at the airport to people who make the metal detector beep. Then they searched our belongings.

"What are you looking for?" I inquired. "What's the big deal about this search? What exactly is it that you're looking for?"

"Radios, cellular phones, and things like that," a deputy said.

"Couldn't you just take our word for it that we're not going to bring any of that stuff? We've been on the outside for a long time now, not listening to the radio, and it was certainly available out there. Isn't our word good enough?"

At that moment, it hit me that Deirdre Robertson and the court had been in charge of us before this moment, and they went out of their way to treat everyone nicely. It may have taken a while to get things done—like the eleven days to get a response to my one letter in November—but everything was done with courtesy. For example, Judge Ito always called us "Ladies and Gentlemen of the jury." Now we had been turned over to the sheriff deputies.

In all fairness to the sheriff's department, deputies are trained to work with criminals and potential criminals. Let's face it: The only people who get searched are criminals. And this search had that sort of feel about it. Slowly, methodically, the deputies searched everyone and everything.

In and of itself, the search was demeaning. The process made me feel like a prisoner, like I'd done something wrong.

The deputies spared nothing. They looked through pockets. They looked through shoes. They upended neatly packed luggage to get to the bottom of suit-cases. One juror was apparently a neat freak, and he got quite upset at this intrusion. He had everything folded just so in his bags and the deputies went through everything, messing up his neatly folded clothes. This did not sit well. I said to myself, "Now there's a man after my own heart. He's neat and tidy and has everything the way he likes it, and he's in no mood to take any crap about it."

The entire episode however was humiliating. It was as if the deputies were asserting their rank with all the subtlety of dogs marking territory. In no un-certain terms, these individuals, humorless behind their guns, badges, and uniforms, had let us know that they were superior beings. Could there be any doubt about that? They had the absolute right to rifle through our things.

Our word was of no value. Honor and trust, those most precious of human commodities, had no worth on the fourth and fifth floors of this hotel, but we were trusted with the outcome of this case.

Already discouraging, the experience was dehu-manizing, too. Of course, deputies referred to us by our juror numbers, which was proper, but that also had the subtle effect of reminding us who was in charge.

Not surprisingly, we almost immediately began to adopt the role of cons—actually, cons in some grainy, black-and-white movie from the Forties or Fifties, the kind that almost certainly would have made it on the approved list of movies we were still allowed to watch. As the deputies moved through our things, I noticed that other jurors were starting to mumble to one another like hard-timers at Alcatraz, talking low and barely moving their lips. The deputies, meanwhile, kept trying to position themselves to "monitor" our conversations.

It took a while for all those searches, but finally when that was over we headed for our rooms. We were led past a control point in the hotel hallway, which was a station staffed by deputies and equipped with a television monitor split four ways, offering deputies the opportunity to monitor us at various common rooms and halls on the hotel floor. The rooms were assigned according to how you sat in the jury box: 1, 2, 3, and so forth. Since I held Seat 3 in the box, I got the third room.

This was a first-class room in a first-class hotel with a few notable exceptions: no TV, radio, or phone. I also noticed there was no security chain on the door. I called a deputy and said, "Excuse me, my privacy chain is missing."

"I'll go and check on that. I'll be right back."

A few minutes later, another deputy showed up at my door and said, "We took those chains off of all the doors. That's because from now on, you have no privacy. We can come in anytime we want."

"If I'm in the shower, taking a shower, you can come in?" asked one of the female jurors who had walked up and heard the deputy talking.

"Yes. We can come in anytime we want."

When we were assigned our rooms, we were handed a *new* set of rules. I put the papers down and unpacked my three bags—a suitcase, a hanging bag, and the computer case. I travel light and I figured that anything I'd forgotten Judy could bring when I saw her next, whenever that was going to be.

That was a jarring thought. In my room, alone with my few things, I felt decidedly alone. It was different than the feeling of homesickness or lonesomeness one might get on a business trip. If I wanted to call Judy from the road, well, there are pay phones at every train station in America and in all hotels. Here I didn't even have a telephone in my room and would have only limited access each day to a phone that was bound to be "monitored." I had no way to contact Judy, except with the help of the sheriff's department. We were forbidden to see each other. It was unnatural. I unexpectedly missed her, missed her bad.

I hung up the suits and sportcoats I'd brought. Feeling emotionally unsettled but at least somewhat settled with my things, I turned back to the new set of rules. More rules. Another list, another reason to feel yet more unsettled and out of control of my own life. (See opposite page).

Along with the rules, we also received a daily schedule. (See page 66).

Once again, this seemed like the work a day routine at a prison yard. Bit by bit by bit, I actually began to feel like a prisoner. This is a strange process, but when you're treated like a prisoner, you begin to act like one. You start looking for ways to talk to each other surreptitiously or sneak food from the dining room or act out in other ways. And this was the start of the process.

During that first day, there wasn't actually much to do. One of the rooms on the fifth floor had been set up for movies, and so I ducked in there for a bit. The movie was *The River Wild*, starring Meryl Streep. Every time she did something positive, everyone in the room cheered.

A deputy stood with the remote control, finger on the mute button, ready to switch off the sound if anything forbidden popped up. It was impossible to ignore the presence of the deputies. They were everywhere. And that day, they were busy reminding us constantly of rules and more rules. Deputies would issue speeches that would go something like this: "No juror will be allowed to enter the room of any other juror at any time. There will be no exceptions to this rule. If you wish to talk with another juror, you must converse in the presence of one of us. If you need to contact another juror, you can approach the other juror's room door in the presence of a deputy. If that juror comes to the door, you may have a brief

SEQUESTERED

RULES FOR JURORS WHILE STAYING AT THE HOTEL

1. Do not tell your relatives where you are staying.
2. Do not discuss anything related to the case with your relatives.
3. You may only discuss the case after you have heard all the evidence and all jurors are present in the jury room during deliberation.
4. No alcoholic beverages are allowed.
5. One juror per room.
6. Jurors are not allowed to go into other jurors' rooms.
7. While at the hotel, if you need to talk to another juror you must stay in the hallway or go into the T.V. lounge.
8. All jurors will go to breakfast, lunch, and dinner as a group.
9. All jurors will go to the visiting areas as a group.
10. All jurors will go on field trips (the mall, exercise area, etc.) as a group.
11. T.V. and phone time ends at 11:00 pm Sunday through Thursday nights.
12. T.V. and phone time ends at 12:00 am on Friday and Saturday nights.
13. Each juror will receive a 15 minute time allotment, to make phone calls, per phone time.
14. All jurors will be in their rooms by 11:00 pm Sunday through Thursday nights.
15. All jurors will be in their rooms by 12:00 am on Friday and Saturday nights.
16. If you smoke, you are allowed to smoke only in your own room.
17. All key cards for your assigned hotel room will be issued every morning and collected every night before bed time.

Please understand that these rules are formulated to comply with court regulations as they pertain to jury sequestration.

This is needed to preserve the integrity of the jury and maintain a workable environment for all personnel assigned to this case.

Please remember, if you have some form of extreme emergency, feel free to approach any of the deputies with your problem.

Arrangements have been made to try and accommodate any emergency.

JURY SCHEDULE

Monday through Friday

Wake up	0530 hrs.
Breakfast	0615 hrs.
Hygiene time	0715 hrs.
Transport	0745 hrs.
CCB 11th floor jury room	0800 hrs.—0845 hrs.
9th Fl. Court jury room	0845 hrs.—0900 hrs.
Court begins	0900 hrs.
Break	1015 hrs.
Resume	1045 hrs.
Lunch	1200 hrs.
Resume	1330 hrs.
Break	1445 hrs.
Resume	1515 hrs.
Conclude	1630 hrs.—1700 hrs.

Transport back to the hotel at the conclusion of court.

Dinner	1800 hrs.—1900 hrs.
Phone and T.V. time	1900 hrs.—2300 hrs.

Wednesday is the same as above except it will conclude at 1600 hrs.

Friday is the same as above except it will conclude at 1500 hrs.

Saturday and Sunday

Wake up	0730 hrs.
Breakfast	0800 hrs.—0900 hrs.
Activity	0900 hrs.—1230 hrs.
Lunch	1230 hrs.—1330 hrs.
Activity	1330 hrs.—1730 hrs.
Dinner	1800 hrs.—1900 hrs.
Phone and T.V. time	1900 hrs.—0000 hrs.

Schedules are <u>tentative.</u>

conversation. If you wish to prolong the contact with the other juror, you may invite that juror to a common area, such as the video room."

After one such speech, I mentioned the fact that the issue of conjugal visits had been discussed during jury selection.

"Will we in fact have conjugal visits?" I asked one of the deputies.

The deputy got a good laugh out of that one. He said they were "working on it."

During the first day of sequestration, I remember thinking that it seemed as if O.J. Simpson, who was being kept in a nine-foot by seven-foot cell at the Los Angeles County Jail, probably had more privileges than we did. And as I learned later, he could use the phone whenever he wanted and call people without having his every conversation monitored. He could watch any TV programs anytime he wanted. He could have frequent visitors. He honestly had more rights and freedoms and had fewer restrictions than we did as jurors. Think about that. Does that seem like the way it's supposed to be?

Once everyone was unpacked, the deputies corralled and marched us from our rooms on the fifth floor down to the food room on the fourth floor. It was midafternoon and time for lunch. The process of getting us in and arranged had taken a lot longer than expected, but lunch had been planned, and once they planned something, they could not deviate from the plan. So lunch it was. By golly, if it was midnight and the schedule said lunch, lunch it would be. By this time I was hungry.

We lined up outside our rooms. We marched in a line down the stairs. Like prisoners in a chain gang, we followed the deputies down, maintaining a line. An exit door was pointed out to us. "If you open it, an alarm will go off," one of the deputies said.

Arriving at the food room, we got in line. It was buffet style with lots of good food.

There were three round tables with nine place settings, three more seats than the twenty-four of us needed. A fourth table was set up for the deputies. At that first lunch, I recall, everyone sort of sat anywhere. Over the next few meals, different people moved to different tables; I know I sat at least once at all three tables, but after just a few meals, people gravitated to the others with whom they felt most comfortable. And, just like that, I looked up, and we were divided, not intentionally, I don't think, but definitely divided. We would march back and forth as an integrated unit, but when we ate, we were definitely divided by race. We had voluntarily segregated ourselves. The Latinos and whites sat at the center table. The African-American jurors were at a second table. And the African-American alternates were at a third.

❋

Call me naive. Maybe I'm too blind to see it. Perhaps I'm foolishly optimistic. But it surprised and saddened me when I realized that over the course of just those few meals, we had managed to segregate ourselves by race at the dinner table.

How did it happen? It's still amazing to me that it worked out this way.

Everyone was free to sit anywhere, of course. I usually sat at the same table with five or six others, usually Farron Chavarria, Francine Florio-Bunten, and Juror Numbers 19, 1290, and 63. We were all comfortable sitting there, I guess. I enjoyed listening to the ladies talk about shopping and about the food we were eating, what was in this, what was in that. It was interesting to me.

One day I sat down at that table and one of the ladies said to me, "That's my seat."

"Oh, excuse me, I'm sorry," I said, and I moved. "I didn't know we had regular seats," I said to her after I found a new place.

"Well, you're right. We don't. I just . . . this is where I sat before."

"It's OK," I said.

So even at the tables themselves, we worked out where we all belonged. If you think about it, it's a fascinating study in human dynamics.

People found a place in which they were comfortable, and they stayed there. I found a group that I was comfortable being with, and for me, that was it. Ultimately, despite the friction that developed between me and some of the others at the table, we still sat together at meals.

So what does it say that the Latinos and whites ended up with each other at one table, that the black jurors were comfortable with each other at another, and that the black alternates were most comfortable together at a third?

I don't know.

I wasn't snubbing anyone and I wasn't conscious of anyone snubbing me. In my mind, I thought and I still think we had a really great jury. We were a diverse group of people. Some were loud, some quiet, some shy. We were family.

As in any family, you're bound to have personality conflicts. No one sees everything from the same point of view. It's a fact of life.

But, I guess, race is a fact of life as well.

The thing is, I don't consider myself white first and anything else second. I just don't see myself that way; I don't look at others that way. I've never considered myself different from any other person. I have some Native American heritage; that's part of me, but it isn't the entirety of who I am. Far from it. I consider myself American. Plain and simple. I considered every one of us on that jury American, too, and I tried to treat everyone the way I want to be treated. Perhaps there were times I misunderstood others; perhaps there were times I was misunderstood or did not explain myself in the best possible way. But I always treated people the way I wanted to be treated. It goes back to the Golden Rule. I'm not a religious person, but I believe that we are all God's children. We are here on the good earth as a family.

Preferences are a natural thing, but prejudice is poison. It's wrong to see the world through the prism of prejudice. And I think people can learn to see that they're wrong and work toward overcoming prejudice. Consider the growth of a human being. We go from not even being able to crawl to being able to run, to jump, to make accomplishments of all sorts. If some are mired in the pit of prejudice, they can climb out and go about their lives with new understanding and try to treat people the way they would like to be treated. I try to do that. That's why I wholeheartedly believe that most of the intelligent people in this country are past the issue of race. I believe that sincerely. To me, the irrefutable fact that a black man was accused of murdering two white people was not the central issue in the case. It seemed logical that the other jurors would also have framed the case the way I had: Here was a human being charged with murdering two fellow human beings.

When we were first sequestered, I thought the jury's deliberations would be held without regard to race. I'd still like to think that. I don't see where race has a bearing on the case. I don't think it should ever have been brought up. Call me naive, or foolishly optimistic. Maybe I'm just too blind to see.

10

❦

Left Behind

Judy

January 11, 1995

It rained so hard that morning. We slogged through the rain to the secret spot near the baseball stadium. We hefted the bags and there were introductions all around. Then Tracy and I kissed and he disappeared in the rain—my husband, my love, my best friend had gone away to an uncertain place for an undetermined time. And I cried and cried.

When the white vans disappeared, I trudged back to my car. I shook off the rain and sat down and turned on the engine. The tears began and I simply could not stop them.

I cried all the way to work. I didn't know why. I still don't know why. I couldn't put my finger on it, couldn't explain it. Still can't. I guess it finally hit me, at that moment, that they had taken Tracy away, taken him somewhere and I had no idea where he was. I could not call him. I could not mail him a letter. He was completely off the face of the earth. Even his motor vehicle registration and driver's license had been taken out of the state's computers for security reasons. It was as if he no longer existed.

I started the car and aimed it toward work. I continued to cry. I shall never forget driving to work that morning, those forty-five minutes in the rain, crying as much as it was raining.

There was no comprehending it. I couldn't understand it at all. It was just a tremendous feeling of loneliness. I couldn't call him, even if I wanted to—and I certainly wanted to. I couldn't find out if he was all right, if things were OK.

I tried to compose myself. No dice.

I realized this was a feeling I was going to have to live with. This was the way it was going to be. I cried some more.

Not only could I not call him, but if he called me, I had to make certain that I was there at a prearranged time or I would miss him. I knew he would be looking forward to those phone calls, and suddenly I, too, was looking forward to them with incredible anticipation. It hit me then that in a way I was sequestered, too. I knew I had to go to work, but then I'd have to come straight home because he'd be able to call only in the evening. I'd have to carefully plan out my activities. If I had to stay late to take care of business and forgot to tell him, he would call and be disappointed. Of course, I could come and go as I pleased—he could not—and that's not to be minimized. But the feeling that one is locked into a schedule and responsible for being at a certain place at a certain time—that is a burden that is not to be taken lightly, either. The burden of letting him down if I were to fail him was what I worried about. It frustrated me deeply to realize that I could not call him right then to reassure him.

This was a feeling I had never felt before. The only comparable experience is when one of our sons went off to Saudi Arabia to fight in the Gulf War. I knew that I could not call him; I had to wait for him to call. Sequestration didn't appear to be a life or death experience—at least at the time, I had no reason to think it would be—but my feelings upon the departure of my son to war and my husband to jury duty were remarkably similar. It was that same loneliness. When I saw my son before he shipped out, he said, "Mom, you've always been able to tell me that everything is going to be OK. You can't tell me that now." It almost killed me that he was right, that I couldn't tell him that everything would be OK. That's the way I felt when Tracy left: I couldn't say for sure, with absolute certainty, that everything was going to be OK.

What did I fear? Something hard to articulate. My

fear was beyond just Tracy, though I worried for him of course. I worried, too, that someone on the jury or their loved ones would suffer in some dramatic way during and after this trial. I could see that coming. I knew with an absolute certainty, could feel it in my soul, that the psychological impact, the emotional fallout from this case would be intense. I just couldn't see whom it would affect or why.

With my background in psychology and human behavior, I knew that being sequestered would stir strong emotions and prompt those feelings to surface in unpredictable ways. These jurors were going to be isolated. They were going to have their names, their very identities, the core of their selves taken away. In its place would be a number. That would be even more dehumanizing. Also, they were going to be told what to do, when to do it, and where to go while doing it. They were going to feel acutely that they had lost control over even the simplest tasks and, consequently, over their lives. They were going to be living an experience that parallels to being taken hostage or being a prisoner of war, and after it ended, they would be excellent candidates for clinical cases of post-traumatic stress disorder.

That's why, as Tracy and I had prepared for sequestration, I had urged him when he went in to take a notebook, make it into a diary, and write down his feelings. He wasn't going to be able to talk to anybody about his feelings. They were bound to be affecting him significantly, and it was important for him to be able to acknowledge those feelings, not bury them where they could do both short- and long-term damage. Just the act of writing them down would help release him from their grip.

"You know I'm not a writer," he would say to me in the weeks before being sequestered. "I don't like to write things down."

"This is one of those things you really need to do," I would respond, sometimes gently, sometimes forcefully. We had this conversation any number of times, as I prodded him to take a notebook with him to the hotel. "You need to do this because it's really going to help you get through this experience. You're going to be hearing so many different things, going to have so much of your familiar power over your life taken away, that you need this as a catharsis, as a place where you can release all that emotion. If you write down how you are feeling that day, that moment, that instant, about whatever it is, you will find that you'll be able to stay sane. You won't find yourself bubbling in anger. Little things won't get big. You need someplace to vent your feelings. Let that place be that notebook. If you write down what you're feeling and you then tear it right out of the notebook, that's fine. That's enough. You don't need to keep a scrap of it. If you want to keep it all together, that's fine, too. Just get those feelings out. It's not important what you do with the notebook afterward. It's not important that I see it or that you show it to anybody. You should show it to me later only if you feel that you want to. This is for you."

When I dropped him off at the secret spot near the stadium, I knew that he had packed a notebook. It never occurred to me that the notebook could ever bring Tracy trouble. After all, this notebook wasn't about the case. It was about Tracy.

✳

That night, Tracy called me from the hotel. Actually, a sheriff's deputy called and asked for me. The deputy made me say my name and my birthday. Having verified that I was indeed Judy Kennedy by matching the name and date I'd given with the name and date Tracy had supplied, the deputy then delivered a short speech. The essence of that speech was that certain topics about the case were forbidden, that there was a fifteen-minute time limit on calls from the jurors, and that the sheriff's department was monitoring juror calls.

After all that, the deputy put Tracy on the phone.

This was the routine we would soon come to learn for all calls that Tracy placed to me while on the jury. It would come to be a bothersome and familiar, but that night, it simply seemed odd and intrusive.

"I need to read you a list of do's and don'ts," Tracy said, kicking off the call with the list of the seventeen rules given to jurors at the time of room assignment. The sheriff's department had insisted, he said, that all twenty-four jurors read these rules to their family members or significant others.

When he finished, I wasn't sure how to respond. I certainly didn't want to say anything that would violate any court orders.

I was curious, naturally, about the hotel. In these circumstances, who wouldn't be? But, again, I didn't

77

want to inadvertently slip up and ask something I shouldn't.

"Are you comfortable?" I asked. That seemed safe. "Yes."

He said no more, which was unusual in itself. The conversation paused for a moment. My mind was racing. I tried again.

"Is it nice?"

"Yes," he said. Another pause. He added, "I've stayed in places like this before."

It felt so awkward. I didn't know what to say. My natural inclination would have been to ask a bundle of questions: Tell me all about the place. What did you have for dinner? How's the food? How are the other jurors? Is everyone getting along? How did you spend the day? How are you doing? No, really, how are you doing?

I wasn't sure, however, what I could ask. It was all so new and I didn't know what would be proper and what would be forbidden.

"Are you excited about getting started?" I tried again. That question seemed safe.

"Yes," he said, but admitted he had mixed emotions. After all the jurors got their things in their rooms, he said, the deputies had given them all sorts of sets of rules and then counted them off and marched them down to dinner. "There's nothing in the room," he said. "It's bare." He offered a bit more, then said, "I feel lost."

I tried to be reassuring, reminding him that we both agreed that anyone could do anything for three

LEFT BEHIND

months. "Remember?" I said. "Anyone can even stand on their head for three months."

The call went on like this. It was chitchat, nervous chitchat. He knew he was being monitored. I felt I couldn't say anything and didn't want to put him in any jeopardy. It was like meeting someone for the first time and trying to think of something to say.

As we neared the time limit, the conversation petered out. After I hung up, I realized that I was glad to hear from him. I also thought of a thousand other things I wished I'd said, things I wanted to say right then and there, but there was no way for me to reach him.

I didn't sleep very well that night. That call was the point at which both of us realized, if only hazily at first, that this case was going to become a wall between us. We would be living in separate worlds. No longer would it be ours together.

I felt uneasy and scared, but there was nothing I could do about it.

11

℣

Who's Who on the Jury

Tracy

SEAT 1

Juror Number 230, a fifty-year-old divorced black woman from south-central Los Angeles, has held this seat during the entire trial. The newspapers say she works as a vendor, but we understood her to work in an accounting department somewhere. She's well spoken and very bright. She's a real leader, very friendly, and has a nice way with people. She became good friends with Numbers 984 and 98. She often carried a word puzzle book with her to court. When her birthday rolled around during the trial, her friends came by on Family Visiting Day and brought enough food to feed everyone, including the other jurors and their families.

This seat, the one next to the one I had, has been held by three different women. The first was Tracy Hampton, who was dismissed on May 1. Single and a flight attendant, Tracy was once an extra on the soap opera "Days of Our Lives." She was articulate and intelligent but very shy. The process of sequestration really wore her down, and she was apparently dismissed after telling Judge Ito, "I just can't take it anymore." The day after she left the jury, she was rushed to a hospital in Marina del Rey for severe depression according to her own statement on TV.

Farron Chavarria, Number 1427, replaced Tracy Hampton. Farron, twenty-nine, is a real estate appraiser for the County of Los Angeles. She was excused June 5 along with Willie Cravin. In court, she took voluminous notes. Farron used to get a lot of interested stares from people in the audience because of a book she carried to court for a while, one of those self-help books: *When I Say No, I Feel Guilty*. We sat next to each other in court and at meals. There were times I felt that everything I did irritated Farron. She and I did not get along very well, nor did she seem to get along with Willie Cravin or Jeanette Harris and a few others. Farron did get along famously with Francine Florio-Bunten, who took Michael Knox's place. From the start, it seemed that both Farron and Francine—who also was originally an alternate—were angling to be on the regular jury. Both made it. Both ended up being excused.

The third juror to sit in Seat 2 was Number 1492, a twenty-four-year-old African-American woman who loves rap music. One day, I had my CD on in my room, and was listening to classical music. She walked by and said, "What is that noise?" I answered, "That is music," and we laughed. She is also a whiz at computer games, and very bright. When her family visited, they always played games that challenged their minds. Scrabble. Or word games. She routinely whipped the pants off all of them.

SEAT 3

This was my seat. Best in the house. Front row. I could see everything and everyone.

When I was excused, my place was taken by Number 1290, a sixty-year-old white woman. She's a retired gas company worker. She's been on a jury before and has a forceful personality. When I say "forceful," I'm being generous. We did not see eye to eye on almost anything, and it seemed she rarely had anything nice to say about anyone. Once, when we were in the vans coming back to the hotel, and she said something about one of the guys directing traffic into the hotel, called him "Mr. Personality" or something like that. I turned around and said to her, "Don't you ever have anything nice to say about anyone?" She gave me a funny look. She was big pals with Farron and Francine and, like them, was originally an alternate. Also in their group was Number 19, who sat in Seat 4.

SEAT 4

Number 19 is a thirty-two-year-old Latino who has been in this seat since the beginning of the trial. He delivers soda pop for a living. During jury selection, he said Simpson was "a great football player." A little boy, maybe five years old and a real ball of fire, visited him every Sunday. When the visit was over, the little boy would cry. It was heartbreaking to see them have to say good-bye to each other. Number 19 and I got along fine for a while, but then we had words, and things were never the same between us. I think he believed everything Number 1290 told him.

SEAT 5

One of the originals is still here, too. She's Number 984, a thirty-seven-year-old black woman who works in a post office. During jury selection, she said that the low-speed chase was "stupid." She likes detective crime books. She was newly married; her husband was in the military. She is very upbeat, bubbly, boisterous. She has more energy than anyone I've ever seen and finds something funny in almost everything. She likes to laugh a lot, and she has a really loud laugh. I mean loud. I tried not to ride with her in the vans or get close to her in the elevators because those were enclosed places and her laugh got to be so loud. But I did genuinely like her.

SEAT 6

The original was Number 228, a forty-eight-year-old African-American man. The very first day, when everyone was introducing themselves, he said, "I work for Hertz." I said, "What? You work for Hertz and they let you on the jury?" He said, "Yeah. I put it on my form, right there." He was dismissed on January 18 apparently because of the Hertz connection. When Number 228 left, Number 247 took his place. He is a forty-three-year-old stocky African-American man who dresses immaculately, favoring black shirts with a sports coat and tie. He's the one whose clothes were folded so neatly in his suitcase, which makes sense when you learn he was in the Navy. He served in search-and-rescue and morgue details. He also has worked for a radio station. He served as a jury foreman before.

SEAT 7

This belonged to Number 462, Jeanette Harris, until April 5. Jeanette is thirty-eight and an employment interviewer. She and I got along. Or, to be precise, I never had any reason to think that we didn't get along. We did not, however, pal around together. Her best pals were Willie Cravin and Number 1233, the woman who sat right next to her in Seat 8; those three were sometimes joined by Number 984 (Seat 5) and by Number 2179. Jeanette is reserved but always seemed to have her guard up. In court, she put on an exceedingly blank face, but after you got to know her, you realized she was taking everything in and passing judgment on every little thing. And let me tell you this: She has a stare that penetrates right through you. She was dismissed because she failed to reveal a past experience with domestic violence. She then alleged in a TV interview that there was racial tension on the jury and that some sheriff's deputies showed favoritism toward whites. She was also reported to have said that despite Judge Ito's orders, jurors were discussing the case. Later, after being called in by the judge, she denied that she'd ever said such a thing. In all my time on the jury, I never, ever heard any of the jurors discussing the case. Never.

A forty-four-year-old single African-American woman, Number 795, now sits in Seat 7. She repairs computers and printers for Superior Court. She and my wife became friendly on visit days. In jury selection, she said, "If I'm not picked, I can look at it and say, 'They let a good one go.'" She always did seem very conscientious. She'll do a good job.

SEAT 8

Another one of the original jurors, Number 1233 is a thirty-eight-year-old single African-American woman who works as an environmental health specialist. Her dad was a police officer. She's quiet. Church-oriented. She doesn't smile much, but when she does, her whole face lights up. One of the sweetest smiles you'll ever see. Big pals with Jeanette Harris and Willie Cravin.

SEAT 9

Number 98 is a fifty-two-year-old African-American woman who has been there from the start. She works for the post office. During jury selection, she described Mr. Simpson as "only human." Her group included Number 230 and Number 984. They got to be such a familiar sight that I called them the Three

Musketeers. Number 98 is sweet. Literally. Once in a while they'd have candy in the jury room. She knew I loved Hershey bars with almonds, and if she ever saw one in the bowl, she'd say, "Oh, they got one of your chocolate bars!" and fish it out for me. She also loved to play cards, especially solitaire. She knew three or four variations of solitaire and taught me a couple of them.

SEAT 10

Trying to keep track of who has been in this seat is a bit like following a game of musical chairs. Four different people have occupied this seat.

Originally it went to Number 320, a thirty-eight-year-old female, a postal carrier. She turned out to be one of the first two people kicked off the jury. She was dismissed on January 18, before opening statements had even begun, because she had been allegedly abused mentally and verbally by an ex-boyfriend since being put on the jury. But when she left, we had no idea why she'd been replaced. It was that way with all four jurors who were excused before me: Number 320; Number 228, who worked for Hertz and was dismissed the same day as Number 320; Catherine Murdoch, who was excused on February 7; and Michael Knox, who was dismissed on March 1. I was sorry to see all the jurors who left before me, especially Number 320. She used to sit next to me at the dinner table. I liked her.

Next in Seat 10 was Number 2017, Catherine Murdoch. She's a sixty-three-year-old white woman. She and I were friends, but she left the jury before we all knew that much about her. She liked to walk fast and eat healthy and she always complained about the food not being healthy.

Willie Cravin, Number 1489, replaced her. I liked Willie. He is a fifty-five-year-old African-American man, a former Navy medic who once worked in the psychiatric ward of the Veterans Administration Hospital in Brentwood, less than a mile from the site where Nicole Brown Simpson and Ron Goldman were killed. Now he's a postal operations manager. Willie is a big, burly man, and he got hung with the nickname Coach because we used to throw a football around. That ended because the deputies were afraid someone would get hurt. Willie is religious, strong-willed, and outspoken. He clashed with Francine Florio-Bunten and Farron Chavarria. His best pals were Jeanette Harris and Number 1233. I liked hanging around with him, though, especially in the movie room. He liked people to be quiet while he was watching a movie, and if he was in there, I knew I could watch in peace and quiet.

Willie was dismissed on June 5. His place was taken by Number 2179, a twenty-eight-year-old African-American woman. She is very bright and has a real thing for crossword puzzles. She's sweet, really nice, and very quiet, and will be a good juror.

SEAT 11

Number 63, a twenty-two-year-old white female, holds this seat. She's been there from the start. She has been in California only for a short time and had a job handling insurance claims. While the trial was going on, she got a raise—she thought that was phenomenal. She used to exercise with Francine Florio-Bunten, Farron Chavarria, and Numbers 19 and 1290. A good juror.

SEAT 12

Michael Knox, Number 620, was here first. Michael is a forty-six-year-old African-American who worked for Federal Express. He was probably the perfect driver for one of their trucks because he is so high-energy. He always seemed to be in motion, full of chatter, eager to be friends with everyone. He is also a musician and I would often walk by his room and hear him thumping away at something, keeping some beat.

He was dismissed on March 1. Taking his spot was Number 353, Francine Florio-Bunten. She was an expert in food, especially Italian food, and an avid shopper. She loved to look at catalogs. Although I thought that we got along all right, I've since learned that was not so. I knew that she and Willie Cravin did not get along.

Francine was excused on May 26, and Number 2457, a seventy-one-year-old African-American woman, took her place. She's been married for forty-two years and is a proud woman, which we all learned during jury selection when she described herself as a "retired cleaning officer." She also said in jury selection that she "never heard of no O.J. Simpson" and never reads anything "except the horse sheet." She used to play one of those electronic blackjack games constantly. She is also a heavy cigarette smoker.

ALTERNATE JURORS

Number 165 is a seventy-two-year-old African-American man who works as a security guard. He said during jury selection that he had experienced "many racial incidents," including one involving a white gang. One time when we were talking, he brought up the fact that he'd been around a few years and remembered when blacks had to ride in the back of the bus. "Wait a minute," I said to him. "I had nothing to do with that. And if you want to get down to it, my ancestors on one side of my family were Native Americans and weren't even allowed on the bus." He thought about that for a moment and then said, "Yeah, man, you're right." And we shook hands.

The other alternate is Number 1386, a twenty-four-year-old white female who works as a fire department receptionist. She used to be a manicurist and personifies the term *big hair*. She always had a good hair day, except for one time when we were summoned to the court on short notice for a session in the evening. She was not at all happy about that, apparently because she hadn't done her hair the way she wanted it. She always made sure that the deputies woke her up early in the morning so that she'd have enough time to do her hair properly. She is married to a black man and said in jury selection that there is a "somewhat serious problem" of discrimination against blacks in Southern California. Her husband is a bodybuilder and one of the nicest guys you'd ever want to know. When asked her reaction to finding out she was in the jury pool, she said, "It was, like, wow!"

From the very beginning, as soon as the jury was selected, I was thinking about who would make a good foreman.

I was certain of only one answer. Not me.

At no point did I want to be the foreman. Never. I never angled for the job, never played backroom politics, never put the full-time press on the other jurors to make me foreman. Not even a wink or a nod. Just wasn't interested.

To begin with, I always thought the foreman should be a woman. Nicole Brown Simpson was the obvious target of this horrible crime and I felt a woman should be the voice of the community passing judgment on her killer. The foreman also, I thought, ought to be a representative of the jury. Given that the jury was composed primarily of African-Americans and of women, it made more sense to me that a female get the job.

Then there is the issue of race. I was the only white man on the entire jury. Given the intense sensitivity to race in Los Angeles as well as the significance the issue assumed in some quarters during the trial, I did not think that I was a suitable candidate for foreman. It made little sense for a white man to act as a leader and public spokesman for a group made up mostly of blacks. These things ought not to matter. But they do.

Don't think, by the way, that I am, even for one second, minimizing the murder of Ron Goldman or the horrific way in which he was killed. But, it seemed to me, he was simply in the wrong place at the wrong time. It always seemed that the killer was focused on Nicole Brown Simpson.

Whatever the verdict, I always felt that the foreman would be asked to explain what happened in deliberations, the hows and whys of the judgment. I did not want that spotlight nor the notoriety that would entail. I don't even like the sound of my voice on tape or the way I look on TV, and I wasn't the least bit interested in being the focus of all that attention. I sincerely wanted to serve and then return to anonymity.

Early on, I made that clear to the others. A group of the ladies on the jury were standing around and I took the opportunity to say, "I know it's awfully early, but I think you ought to be thinking about who's going to be the foreman, and I think it should be a female." Another time I approached Michael Knox because it looked to me that he was trying to be everyone's buddy, and I figured he was politicking for the foreman's job.

"Let's talk a minute," I said to Michael. We walked out of the earshot of the other jurors, and I said to him, "Michael, I think a female should be the foreman."

"Well, I think everyone should make up their own minds," he replied.

"Hey, OK, whatever you think. I just want to let you know: I do not want the foreman's job."

"Well," he said, "I do."

I let it go at that. And it became a moot point after Michael was dismissed in March.

Among the jurors still remaining on the panel, the woman who replaced me, Number 1290, served on a jury before. Naturally, some might think she should be the foreman; after all, she's been through deliberations before. But others have also had prior jury service: Numbers 247 and 795. But I always thought that Number 230 in Seat 1 would make an excellent foreman. She's articulate and friendly and enjoys the confidence of the other jurors. She's always been my first choice.

12

Culture of Paranoia

Tracy

Much has been made about the allegation leveled by Jeanette Harris after she was dismissed from the jury that certain deputies were racist. I never saw evidence of that. Rather, my impression was that they were equal opportunity oppressors with a rigid, almost slavish, adherence to rules and routine.

They were the enforcers of a schedule that was a leading cause of the culture of paranoia that consumed the jury. After just a few days, we began to call them "the overseers."

The printed "jury schedule" that we were given when we first arrived at the hotel barely hinted at the rigors of the daily routine.

Wake-up was at five-thirty each weekday morning. An overseer would knock on your door.

On the original schedule, breakfast was at a quarter past six. That got changed to six sharp. We had to line up, outside our doors, on each side of the hallway. They'd count noses. When everyone was there, we'd line up and walk downstairs to breakfast.

As a matter of fact, anytime we went anywhere or did anything, we lined up and marched. Well, sort of. But in a line.

In the beginning, the rule was that everyone had to go to every meal. Even if you didn't eat, you had to sit there and watch everyone else. That was an uncomfortable and stupid situation. It was especially ridiculous at breakfast, since very few jurors were morning people and there was always food available at the courthouse.

About seven-ish, we'd come back upstairs. Between seven forty-five and eight, we'd line back up again in the hall. It was time to "go to work."

The overseers had it in their minds that we had to be at the courthouse by eight. I asked the lead deputy one morning why that was, especially since court did not begin until nine at the earliest. He said, "I have to get O.J. taken care of first." We would line up in the hallway, go downstairs to the vans with the tinted windows, and go from there to the courthouse via a basement entrance. These elevators were the freight elevators used for trash and Lord knows what else. They smelled bad. Up to the eleventh floor we'd go, all of us plus two deputies, sometimes four. There, we had to wait all crammed into one elevator, until all the overseers stepped out to check the hallway, the stairs, and the doors for unauthorized people.

One time, I stepped out when the doors opened on the eleventh floor and an overseer ordered, "Get back in here!"

"For what?" I said.

"We may have to close the doors and leave this floor in an emergency."

"What emergency?"

"That's for us to determine."

Another time, one of the ladies in the back of the elevator got motion sickness and said, "I have to get out. I have to get out." At first, the answer was no. After a few moments and some complaints, common sense prevailed and they relented.

Once the perimeters of the back hallway of the eleventh floor of the courthouse were deemed secure, we'd go from the elevators to what we called the "food room," which was three times the size of the jury room, where plenty of food was always on hand. In the mornings, snacks, Danishes, cereal, milk, and fresh fruit were available. There was an abundance of food. No one could possibly go hungry. In fact, at the beginning people were complaining that they were eating too much and not getting enough exercise.

What there weren't enough of were chairs. There were four tables and four chairs at each table.

"Did anyone take high school math?" I asked one of the overseers upon seeing the food room for the first time. "It doesn't add up. There are more of us than there are chairs."

The overseer replied, "Well, you can sit down. There are sofas."

A couple months later, another table and four more chairs arrived.

"Well, you finally got another table," that overseer said to me.

Though two jurors were gone by then, the math still didn't add up, but I quit complaining.

The food room also contained three sofas. Three people max could sit on each sofa. So we could squeeze in, more or less, but sitting on the sofa with a plate of food in your lap was a challenge.

For a week or so after we were first sequestered, we made it only as far as the food room. The lawyers apparently were wrangling over who knows what, so we sat there and ate and ate and ate. The rain outside never seemed to let up and, inside, each day seemed like an eternity. People were getting on one another's nerves. There were personality clashes over small things like someone laughing too loud or telling a joke that offended someone or being accused of staring at others. Take that many strangers crammed together in close quarters and behind locked doors, and you're bound to have conflict. Imagine looking at the same faces, day after day, and having nothing to say to any of them. Keep in mind, we could not talk about the case or what went on in the courtroom because it was likely to be overheard by an armed deputy.

After just a couple days like this, someone would

say to one of the overseers before we left the hotel: "Is today going to be like yesterday?"

The response would be something like, "We don't know anything. We're just supposed to get you over there."

It was tremendously liberating the next week, when we finally started going down to the ninth floor, where Judge Ito's courtroom is located. But that was a short- lived thrill. It, too, quickly became a part of the monotonous routine.

About nine most mornings, when it was time to go to court, one of the overseers would say, "OK, we're ready," or, "OK, let's go," or, "Head 'em out." Once, I remember, we heard, "Ladies and gentlemen . . ." which was a refreshing change.

We'd head out of the food room and go back into the freight elevator, down to nine. Again, we'd have to stay in the elevator until the overseers had given the all-clear sign. We'd come out through the hall-way, past a door, through the main hallway in the courthouse and into the courtroom, then through to the jury room behind the courtroom itself.

We knew when we were back in the jury room that there were things going on in that courtroom that we were not privy to. Motions, that kind of thing. So we would wait and wait and wait and of course we got impatient and frustrated. We wanted to get to work.

In the jury room there were puzzles and cards. At first people would either play them or chitchat about kids and food or whatever you talk about in a room full of strangers. As the trial wore on, the chatter all but disappeared. More and more people would sit in the jury room and reflect unto themselves about the goings-on. We weren't supposed to form an opinion until all the evidence had been presented. Absolutely no one ever expressed an opinion about the case, but people got quieter and quieter in that jury room as time went by. They played solitaire, read, or just stared out the window.

At some point, the door would open and someone would announce, "OK, they're ready," and we would file back into the courtroom.

We all knew into what order we had been placed in the jury box, so we would walk out in line according to the seat number. That way we wouldn't all be in the way of one another at the entrance to the box. In theory, that was the way it was supposed to work. Quite often, someone would trip over someone's shoes or bang someone else's chair. It proved to be a serious sore spot which grew worse as time went on.

At the noon break, it was back to the elevators and the eleventh floor. Not once did we have to wait even a minute for the food, which was always catered and consistently excellent. It was all-you-could-eat, but I always tried to eat a light lunch so I wouldn't get sleepy in the courtroom in the afternoon. I wanted to be sure to pay close attention. If you've ever been in a courtroom in the afternoon, you know how tempting it can be to close your eyes and nod off.

After our meal, some people stayed at the tables playing cards, talking, or reading the cut-up newspapers. We had two copies of the *Los Angeles Times*, the *Daily News*, *USA Today*, and, occasionally, the *Wall Street Journal*. Any possible reference to the case was cut out, which often left you holding a piece of newspaper that looked like a second grader had used it for a papier-mâché project. You got a feel for the dimensions of O.J. mania when you'd pick up *USA Today* and half the paper would be gone.

After lunch I preferred to doze just a bit. I would try to claim one of the sofas, put my feet up, and close my eyes.

I'd be awakened by the call: "OK, we're ready." Back to the ninth floor, through the courtroom, to the jury room. Usually, though, they weren't ready for us, and we would wait until two or three, even four in the afternoon. If things started on time, at one-thirty, we'd finish between four-thirty and five except on Fridays, when court ended at three, and Wednesdays, which was a family visiting day, when the session would end at four.

If it was a visiting day, we'd meet with family at the courthouse for a couple of hours. If not, it was back to the food room for an hour or so. After that, back to the vans and the hotel.

At six, we would line up outside our rooms for dinner.

The food was consistently excellent. In fact, it was too good too rich and there was always way too much of it. Always two or three main courses for dinner. The menu was on a two-week rotation, however. If it was Salisbury steak on Tuesday night, you'd know it would be Salisbury steak two Tuesdays from then. Chicken was a constant on the menu. They served a lot of fish, too—probably every other day. Lasagna was a regular. Mixed vegetables, too. The public, I think, had visions of us ordering from a menu. We ate the same food the hotel employees ate.

Desserts were often elaborate—a lot of parfaits in glasses, always topped with a strawberry. Strawberries were a theme. They showed up on virtually every dessert one way or another.

After dinner, the overseers would sometimes let us go out on a secured patio on the fourth floor where we could walk or jog around if it wasn't too congested with the other jurors.

No one would quarrel with the idea that exercise was a good idea, especially with all the stress we had weighing on us. But who thought up the idea that exercise time ought to be immediately after dinner? No way could anyone work out or work up a sweat on a full stomach.

Initially we had been told that we could use the exercise room that the hotel made available to all its guests, but only after ten at night, when it was closed to the other guests, or before six in the morning. Then we were told that the exercise room was essentially off-limits between four and six in the morning because the hotel needed those two hours to clean the room.

Ultimately, after rooms opened up with the dismissal of a few jurors, we got our own workout room on the fifth floor. That was the good news. The bad news: Predictably, like the VCR room, it became a source of conflict.

For me, a workout room wasn't the answer. I preferred to keep to the routine I had at home, which was out of bed at five each morning and out for a run. To do that, I had to convince one or more of the overseers to hop out of a warm bed and keep me company. A hit-or-miss kind of deal.

My other conflict with exercise time on the patio was that phone time began at seven P.M. in the evening. Normally, Judy would get home by seven, and I always wanted to talk to her as soon as I could. But there were an incredible number of hoops you had to jump through to make a call.

For starters, there were only four phones available to us. Four phones in a room about 15 by 15 feet. The phones were on small round tables lined up in a row. All the tables that were available to us at either the hotel or the courthouse were round, never square, never with sharp corners. An overseer was always on hand inside the room. Sometimes there were several overseers in or around the room; I once counted six. Sometimes they would play cards with each other, but it was obvious they were listening to your calls.

You couldn't just pick up a phone and dial. The deputies had a sheet on which they filled out the juror's number, the number being called, the time the call was put through, the time the connection was made, and the time the call was completed. A call could not last more than fifteen minutes.

Given all the information the overseers were recording, it seemed logical to me that they were taping all the calls. That way, if something unexpected happened, they could go back and figure out who called who and what was said.

That might seem paranoid. But there was ample reason to feel paranoid. Each of us had in essence surrendered his or her identity; to the overseers we were numbers. In each call, after verifying that it was indeed Judy on the line, a deputy would say, "I'm Deputy So-and-So. This call could be monitored or is monitored. Don't talk about the case. You have Juror Number 602 calling you."

Since the case was off-limits as a subject and the case was what I was immersed in, our calls were awkward. But, let's face it, the circumstances did not exactly lend themselves to intimacy. Who wants to say "I love you" with a bunch of overseers listening in? You could just tell their ears would perk up. They're human, too, and it's human nature to talk about other people. Since I overhead them talking about different jurors and their families, I'm sure they talked about us.

The calls lasted exactly fifteen minutes. Not a minute longer. A couple times an overseer said to me, "Hey, your time is up." If you wanted to, you could then get back on the list for another call, but there was no guarantee if you'd get phone access again that night.

If you weren't one of the first four people in line when the phone room opened at seven, there was no telling what time you'd get to make a call. You had to put your number on a waiting list. When your number came up, you'd be retrieved, either by the person who'd just hung up the phone or by an overseer, if that overseer was feeling obliging, which wasn't very often. There were times when my number would be scratched off the list and I'd have to start all over again at the bottom.

Besides the phone, the only other thing to do in the evenings was to catch a movie. When we were first sequestered, our floor included a phone room, a movie room, and a game room. The movie room featured the movies that were available through the hotel's TV system. We didn't have a VCR, so we went through the movies pretty quickly.

We asked the overseers if we could have a VCR. No can do, they said.

So someone wrote a letter to Judge Ito asking if we could have a VCR. Ridiculous. Someone besides Judge Ito could have made that decision. But he had to do it. Little things like this ought to be handled by someone else; it's a waste of his time. Apparently, he decided we could have a VCR, because one appeared. Then we were faced with the issue of what movie to watch. We had to take votes each night. Say it was a choice between *The Flintstones* and *True Lies*. Whichever movie got the most votes was the one we'd see.

When the movie was over, it was time for bed. Time, that is, for yet another drill.

You were supposed to go to the Control Point in the hallway and tell the overseer there that you were ready for bed. A deputy was supposed to walk with you to your room, hand you the key, watch you open the door, make sure you actually entered the room, retrieve the key from your hand, and then stay there until he or she made sure that the door was closed.

The next day, there'd be a knock on the door at five-thirty A.M. and we'd get up and do it all over again.

It was brutal. Eventually, Francine Florio-Bunten

wrote Judge Ito a note: "I just can't stand the rigors of sequestration. It is driving me nuts."

If you were to think about being locked in a hotel room, it probably wouldn't seem like such an awful ordeal. The normal person would say, "Ah, no big deal. I've been in hotel rooms before. They're OK. And they give you those neat little bottles of shampoo and conditioner for free."

Now imagine you can get into the hotel, but you can't get off the floor during the evening. There was no hanging out in the bar or checking out the scenery. At night, once you turned in, you couldn't leave. There's no phone. There's no radio. The TV is there but it's not connected.

What else is there to do in a hotel room? It may be plush and it may be nice and it has swell curtains and a view out the window, but it becomes a prison after a while and that's exactly how you come to think of it.

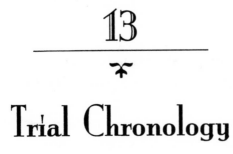

13

Trial Chronology

January 11–January 18, 1995

Wednesday
January 11, 1995
1st day of sequestration

• The twelve jurors and twelve alternates began their sequestration at an undisclosed location.

Jury not present

• In court the domestic violence issues were argued by both sides before Judge Lance Ito, with no jury present. The prosecution, represented by Deputy District Attorney Lydia Bodin, detailed a long history of incidents involving abuse of Nicole Brown Simpson by O.J. Simpson. Included were numerous representations of physical and mental abuse extending over the seventeen years of their relationship.

• The defense, with argument by Gerald Uelmen, sought to exclude evidence of "domestic discord" citing inadmissibility as hearsay, irrelevance, unreliability and that the prejudicial impact outweighed the probative value.

Thursday
January 12, 1995
2nd day of sequestration
Jury not present

• The prosecution withdrew eighteen of the original sixty-one alleged abuse incidents previously recounted, as perpetrated by O.J. Simpson upon Nicole Simpson.

• Prosecutors advanced the theory that Ronald Goldman was killed because O.J. Simpson believed Goldman was romantically involved with Nicole Brown Simpson.

• Prosecution called witness Donald Dutton, an expert on domestic violence, to testify.

• Famed criminal attorney F. Lee Bailey, sixty-one, made his first appearance for the defense team, as he cross examined Donald Dutton, the lone prosecution expert at this hearing.

Friday
January 13, 1995
3rd day of sequestration
Jury not present

• The race issue dominated as Deputy District Attorney Christopher Darden and defense lawyer Johnnie Cochran, Jr., both African-Americans, engaged in an emotional exchange. The two lawyers took opposing views on playing the race card, prior to the expected testimony of Detective Mark Fuhrman.

• Two jurors were dismissed by Judge Ito, although the jury remained sequestered. A thirty-eight-year-old Latina postal worker from Norwalk and a forty-eight-year-old African-American employed by Hertz Corporation were excused from further service following an investigation of jury misconduct the judge had earlier instigated.

Saturday
January 14, 1995
4th day of sequestration

Sunday
January 15, 1995
5th day of sequestration

Monday
January 16, 1995
6th day of sequestration
Court not in session

• A reported rift in the O.J. Simpson defense team apparently came to a head during the weekend, only days before opening statements were scheduled to begin. The controversy involved Robert Shapiro and F. Lee Bailey, the two longtime friends who had a personal as well as an attorney/client relationship. Bailey is the godfather of Shapiro's oldest son, and in 1982, Shapiro represented Bailey on a drunk-driving charge.

Tuesday
January 17, 1995
7th day of sequestration
Court not in session

• Opening statements expected to begin today were rescheduled for Thursday, January 19.

• In a motion unsealed today, prosecutors stated that O.J. Simpson had hit his first wife, Marguerite Simpson Thomas, approximately twenty years ago, necessitating a call to the police. The statement of L.A.P.D. Officer Terry G. Schauer, who responded to the call, was attached to the motion.

• Judge Ito announced that opening statements scheduled to begin tomorrow morning will again be delayed. Monday, January 23, is the new start-up date.

Outside of court

• The defense team, thought to be in internal disarray, made a show of solidarity by coming to court side by side, arm in arm, in lock step. The two lawyers who have apparently come to a parting of the ways are long time friends F. Lee Bailey and Robert Shapiro. Shapiro released information to the media about the rift after accusing F. Lee Bailey of leaking defense information. It has become noticeable that Robert Shapiro is deferring to Johnnie Cochran, who will now take the leading role in the trial for the defense.

Wednesday
January 18, 1995
8th day of sequestration
Jury present

• Judge Lance Ito officially dismissed two jurors and replaced them with randomly drawn alternates. All the jurors arrived at court together, but the two were excused separately out of hearing of the panel. The two alternates, a white female, sixty-three, who is a legal secretary at the law firm of Gibson, Dunn & Crutcher, and an African-American male, forty-three, who works as a marketing representative, were seated.

• Jurors asked for and received permission for conjugal visits.

Jury not present

• In an important decision, Judge Ito ruled that much of the domestic violence evidence will be admitted. Thus the prosecution will be able to address the pattern of abuse in their opening statements.

• Any relative of a victim will be excluded from the courtroom when another family member is testifying, if that relative is going to testify about the same matter.

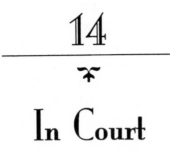

14

In Court

Tracy

January 18, 1995

After a week of waiting, Wednesday was finally showtime. We all put on suits and dresses and filed into the jury box. This was our first appearance in the courtroom since we'd arrived at the hotel and, I confess, it felt good to have some purpose.

As we walked in, every eye in the courtroom turned toward us. A once-in-a-lifetime sensation. This was history in the making, and I'd been granted a front-row seat.

On TV it appears that the courtroom is formidable.

The wood walls. The great seal of the state of California. In real life, the courtroom is actually fairly small. Everyone is packed together—the jury and the lawyers in front of the railing, behind it the press and the spectators. Judge Ito is the only one with any room to spread out. He even has room on his desk for coffee cups and knick-knacks, which consist of a collection of old-fashioned hourglasses.

After I took my seat, I gazed around, surveying the scene. There he was, across the room: O.J.

We'd seen him before in court, during jury selection, but the reality of it hit me again at that moment, hit me hard. He was charged with murder. I'd been charged with judging him. It was a responsibility of enormous proportions. Again, I pledged to myself to do my best.

O.J. looked over each and every one of the jurors and alternates. It was as if he was speaking silently with each of us in turn. He looked at me. I looked back. Our eyes locked momentarily . . .

It's said that O.J. Simpson has charm. He does. That he has charisma. He certainly does. He has a self-confidence that radiated about the room. Ordinarily, O.J.'s celebrity did not affect me, but in that instant he was mesmerizing. This was the man who had supposedly butchered two people? Could that be possible? He was so affable, so poised, so likable.

I thought I detected a small smile pass across O.J.'s face. I had to look away. He moved on to others in the box. I looked to my left. Behind the bar was a gaggle of reporters, all pressed together, furiously scribbling in their notebooks. They were watching us

watch O.J. Each and every one of them was monitoring us, looking for clues of any sort. Sketch artists
were recording our every twitch. Incredible. It felt
odd to be the focus of such scrutiny. What were they
so intently scouring our faces, our dress, our manner-
isms for? Was it for signs of weakness? Had we done
something wrong? Was it me? Had I done something
wrong?

Judge Ito launched into a speech. ". . . welcome
you, ladies and gentlemen of the jury . . ."

The judge made a few remarks and outlined a few
more general guidelines. He told us that two of the
jurors were being replaced. Out were Number 320 in
Seat 10, and Number 228, the man who had worked
for Hertz in Seat 6. In were two of the alternates,
Number 2017 and Number 247.

The judge then grilled us about our exposure to
news reports about the trial. Had we seen or read or
heard anything we weren't supposed to? One of the
alternates said she had seen a photo of a bruised and
battered Nicole Brown Simpson on the front of the
National Enquirer while in line at the market. The
judge said the photo was a "phony" and the alternate
said it would have no impact on her view of the case.

Given the opportunity for a dialogue with the
judge, several of us piped up about a topic that was
much on my mind: conjugal visits. I was glad to
know that others were interested, too. Some people
broached the topic with delicacy, mindful that the
press was listening. I opted for the direct approach.

"I would like you to reconsider or to consider conjugal visits," I said as the whole world watched and listened.

"I have already reconsidered that and have directed the sheriff to make arrangements for that," Ito responded.

That brought smiles all around.

�

Back at the hotel, the overseers informed us that the first conjugal visit would be that Saturday, the twenty-first, and that we'd have five hours with our spouse or our significant other. I made sure to get phone time that night to call Judy. She was off on a business trip the next day and I wanted to make sure she'd be back in town by Saturday night. If all went well, she said, she was due back Saturday afternoon. A million things could go wrong. Flights get delayed all the time. People get bumped. The weather could stay awful. It was her very first trip with her new job. Who knew if things would go smoothly? There was nothing I could do about any of it.

But I missed her and I needed to see her.

As I wandered the halls that evening, the loss of the two jurors who'd been excused was noticeable. I wondered if others noticed, too.

When the guy from Hertz was let go, I figured maybe the Hertz connection had something to do with it. I didn't know. I had no idea why the other woman was suddenly gone. We had no time to prepare for the loss, but it told me that you really couldn't get close to anyone; you couldn't risk the

114

emotional investment. That's the way they wanted it, I guess.

On one hand, they wanted you to be close. They crammed you together and you did everything together and developed that sense of togetherness. On the other hand, they didn't want you to be close because they wanted diverse opinions on the jury. And if you started going everywhere together and doing everything together, subtlely you became a single entity instead of individuals.

It was a tension I felt acutely that night.

I also felt powerfully how fragile one's existence on the jury could be. What had cost these two their seats? I had no firm answers. What conduct put you at risk? Again, no answers.

That creeping sense of paranoia—there it was again.

✻

An immediate consequence of the dismissal of the two jurors was that two of the rooms on the fifth floor of the hotel were free.

Tracy Hampton, who had a room right next to where the deputies congregated, had been complaining that their radios were keeping her awake, and that their voices were so loud she could hear them all night long. She was also suspicious that her room was being searched. I, too, wondered whether my things were being searched. There was no proof that they were. I simply could not be sure that they were not. After experiencing the way the overseers had proclaimed their unlimited access to our things and their unfettered power over our lives, it would have been foolish to dismiss Tracy's suspicion as unwarranted.

Another one of the ladies wanted to move, too, because she had originally been put in a room specially outfitted for someone who was wheelchair-bound. Everyone had wondered, what's the big deal about a room set up for someone who's disabled? One problem was in the closet. The bar was only half as high as it would ordinarily be. The woman said she couldn't hang anything up properly. Everything she hung up would drop to the floor. She didn't even know the other rooms had standard closets until she talked to others. Even that took her a few days, because she wasn't sure that she could talk about it without breaking the rules. When she finally figured out that she was in a specially outfitted room, she complained to the overseers. "Just hang it double," I overheard them say. "Just fold it up and hang it over the bar so it doesn't hang on the floor." When she asked if she could move, they said no.

After the two jurors were excused, the overseers made a point of telling all of us that none of us could change rooms. "That's the rules. If you don't like it, write a letter." I had learned this lesson back in November. If you wanted anything done, anything at all, you had to write a letter. It did no good to put a complaint in writing and submit it to the overseers. If you wanted to make sure it got the proper attention, it had to be a letter to the judge, personally addressed to him. It got around quickly that our letters saying "We have such and such a problem" weren't getting to the judge unless they were addressed to Judge Ito. We believed that the overseers would open a letter that wasn't personally directed to the judge. We also believed that if the letter involved the overseers, that letter suddenly got lost.

When the two rooms became vacant, the letter writing began in earnest. It usually took what seemed like an eternity to get a response, but this time the two women soon had new rooms.

Score one for our side.

15

Human Touch

Tracy

January 21, 1995

Conjugal visits. Who gets conjugal visits?

That's right. Prisoners.

Before the wardens locked the prisoners away for some good old-fashioned you-know-what, what did we inmates get? The rules and regulations of love.

In our hotel, the law was laid down before any of us were.

A few days before the big night, Deputy Jex, the head deputy, who had a distinct air of authority and whom I actually admired, explained how the conjugal visits would work. He spoke elegant cop-speak in an announcement that went like this: "The conjugal visits will commence at 1900 hours. That's seven P.M. They will have a duration of no more than five hours, ending promptly at midnight. To effect the transportation schedule necessary to meet these parameters, your visitors must be present at the specified pickup point at no later than 1830 hours. That's six-thirty P.M. At that time, deputies will shuttle your visitors here to the hotel. You may greet and spend time with your visitors in the hallway or your room. . . ."

That got a laugh and a few cackles from the group.

Deputy Jex didn't miss a beat: "But for those of you who would prefer to receive your visitors in your rooms . . ."

More laughs.

"Be advised that once you enter your room you must stay there for the duration. There will be no exceptions to this rule and it will be strictly enforced. All visitors will leave the hotel at midnight. There will be no exceptions to this rule and it, too, will be strictly enforced."

I was thinking, "What's the big deal about midnight?" Later, I asked one of the other overseers, "Why couldn't they just spend the night?"

"Well, what are we going to do? Feed them breakfast? If we did, then what are we going to do? Offer room service? Where do we stop? There would be a whole parade of inconveniences, and I don't think we're going to do that."

Ask a question, get an answer.

There were more rules to read to our visitors when

they arrived, and this was in addition to their own set of rules. They'd be informed that conjugal visits were a privilege, not a right. They'd have to swear not to reveal the name or location of the hotel. They could not speak with any juror except the one they were visiting.

And, most importantly, they could not speak about the case during the visit.

This would be the first time I had seen Judy for ten days since that rainy morning at the secret spot near the baseball stadium ten days ago. I had so much to share. I don't think I felt any different from any of the others who were entertaining a guest that night. So what could I talk about? The food, the weather, things like that. I could tell her about the room and the food.

Get real. She'd be curious about the case. It's human nature. Given the many times I had warned her not to discuss the case, though, I didn't think that she'd break that rule. That one was inviolate. Still, this would be the first time we'd be alone, with no deputies monitoring our conversation. Or would the overseers have gone so far as to bug our rooms?

There it was again—that creeping feeling. Were the overseers so twisted, so sick, that they would record and tape the lovemaking of two adults in the privacy of their own room? I had no evidence that the overseers had planted microphones in the potted plant. But I couldn't be sure that they had not, either.

The night Judy was to arrive, I reminded myself to be careful. I wanted to accentuate the positive. This was going to be a great night—no, a great weekend.

We had been told that after the conjugal visit on Saturday night, Sunday would be Family Day. Although we would be at the courthouse for security reasons, we could entertain any member of our family or friends for the afternoon. For me, this meant Judy, but for others, it meant parents, sisters, brothers, kids, grandparents, friends, or whomever. Snacks were available. For the jurors who didn't have partners (one juror's husband couldn't make it that first night), this would be a nice treat.

The clock kept moving closer to seven. Inside my room, I turned on the computer, put a CD in the player, and let the music play. I had special desserts I had brought back from dinner, soft lighting, and music. I looked at the door. I looked at my watch. At the door again. At my watch. I looked out the window. At the door. The watch.

I sat there, eager with anticipation, waiting for the love of my life, and my best friend.

16

✤

A Bad Honeymoon

Judy

January 21, 1995

That first conjugal visit consisted of a series of moments that have to rank among the most bizarre of my entire life. Deputies searched everything I brought, including my lingerie. The experience was similar to what I imagine a call girl would go through. I was searched, and after having sex, I was escorted from the hotel and whisked away to my car.

Tracy tried to make it seem like a honeymoon. I wouldn't wish this kind of honeymoon on anyone.

To make it to the hotel that night, I had to be at

another meeting place at a specific time. I pulled into the garage, parked, looked about, and saw a table. There must have been a half-dozen deputies at this table. They were all male except for one.

I thought: This is for a conjugal visit. They know that. This is uncomfortable and I am embarrassed.

None of the deputies made eye contact. But just the thought that all those men were sitting there and I had to go to them upset me.

They searched everything I brought. I had to show them my driver's license to prove that I was me. I signed a declaration stating that I would not talk about the case. A deputy ran a metal detector wand over me.

Then I was told to go sit in a van until they were ready.

The windows in the van were heavily tinted, so I couldn't really see out. Every couple of minutes, someone else would join me in the van. Talk about an awkward silence. What was there to say?

Eventually there were seven of us in the van. It turned out that the same seven people rode in the van every Saturday night, and we finally did talk to one another. That first night, though, all was quiet. Two drivers who we eventually called Starsky and Hutch got in. They never said a word, just fired up the engine and drove. As the weeks went by, one or two people would try to crack a joke about speeding tickets or something equally inane. But we never heard a peep from Starsky or Hutch.

I didn't watch where we were going. What would have been the point? We pulled into some underground garage and the deputies told us to get out. We stood there like cattle and they said, "Well, go over to the elevator." We didn't know where it was. This was like pushing a rope uphill. They sighed and led us to the elevator. We got to a particular floor. They got out and checked to make sure all was clear. We got out and onto another elevator to another floor. They got out, looked around, and then we got out.

We were lined up in front of this Control Point packed with deputies. Again, all male. I told them my name again. I told them who I was there to see. I felt as if I were yelling, "OK, everybody knows what I'm here for!" It was incredibly humiliating. I didn't look at any of the other visitors; they didn't look at me or at anyone else. All eyes were down.

The deputies told us, "Once you enter the room, you must stay inside. We will knock on the juror's door a few minutes before midnight. You will line up in the hall. Everyone will go back together to the point from which we departed."

I was led down the hall to Tracy's room—My was he happy to see me.

It was as if I were his guest in his own very special place. He had music playing. He had only one light, but he had draped a T-shirt over it, so the light was soft. He showed me the desserts he had brought up from dinner, beautiful desserts in stemmed glasses.

I brought out some sparkling grape juice and two little wine glasses. No alcohol. That was a juror no-no.

So we tried to make it like a second honeymoon. Or like a tryst between two lovers captivated by an unquenchable passion and driven to check into one of the better hotels in town.

This was not, however, the stuff of romance novels.

For one thing, Tracy was chattering away. He was far more animated than usual. To use a Southern expression, he was like a monkey on a hot rake. He flipped from place to place. I was alarmed to see him so hyper. As the weeks went by, he would become even more animated, even more severely hyper.

Though he was bouncing around the room, I noticed that first night that he also seemed unusually withdrawn. He didn't have much to say. And what he did say, he said in a whisper. Then again, I confess that I was a bit paranoid that first night, too. We looked at each other and I said, "Is the room bugged? Is there a camera in here somewhere?" I could not put the thought out of my mind. It made me very tense. There was a picture above the bed and I thought, that would be the best place to put a bug. We both started to whisper to each other. There was no reason to whisper, we just did.

✄

Since we had five hours with each other, I figured that not every minute was going to be spent in passionate embrace. I had just gotten back that afternoon from my trip to Chicago. I had never been there before and was eager to share my experiences with Tracy, so I brought along a map of Chicago. I showed him where I'd stayed and how close that hotel was to my business meetings, where I'd walked and had dinner. "Next time you go," he said, "I want you to go to the Sears Tower," and then he showed me on the map where it was located.

I'd also brought a map of Los Angeles. It was just one of those rent-a-car maps that you get at the airport, and in my haste to get to Tracy's hotel, I'd just stuffed it into the duffle bag along with the map of Chicago. "We had an outing," Tracy said, picking up the L.A. map. "Let me show you where it was because I'd like for us to go there, too. It's a beautiful place." He drew a little star on the map at the spot where they'd had an afternoon outing at the beach. "We really need to go because they have cute shops and stuff like that," he said, lightly touching the map.

When I had checked into the hotel where Tracy was staying, these maps were at the very top of my duffle bag. The deputies took them out, looked at them, and put them back. It was a natural thing for me to take maps to Tracy. We're map people and it was sweet that evening to share them. When I left I thought it would be nice to leave the maps behind as a reminder of how we liked to share our good times together.

A couple of minutes before midnight, there was a knock on the door. We all lined up in the hallway. It was really funny. Everyone was lined up and all heads were down, eyes looking at the floor. Some people were just kicking their feet or stubbing their toes against the carpet. No one wanted to make eye contact with anyone. Each person knew why the others were there and, presumably, what the others had done. No one looked at anyone. The embarrassment was mortifying.

So there we were, lined up side by side. A deputy announced, "OK, let's go." They took us to the elevators and we went winding back down again, back into the garage and the vans and then out onto the streets and to the place where we had parked. I got out, turned the ignition key in my own car, and thought, thank goodness that's over.

17

❦

Family Visits

Judy

January 22, 1995

The next day, as usual, there was a routine to follow.

I'd been told to be at the courthouse between one-thirty and two in the afternoon. I'd also been warned not to be even a minute late.

The place we'd been assigned to park was a couple of blocks from the courthouse in downtown Los Angeles, behind what's come to be known as Camp O.J., with all the scaffolding and TV trucks and satellite dishes across the street from the main entrance to the Criminal Courts Building.

When I pulled up to the lot, I didn't want to say anything I would get in trouble for, so I said to the guard, "I'm supposed to be at the Criminal Courts Building between one-thirty and two," figuring she knew I was one of the O.J. jury visitors. Why else would anyone come to downtown Los Angeles on a rainy Sunday in January to go to the Criminal Courts Building?

"What for?" she replied.

"Well, I was just told to come here to park," I said.

"I'm sorry," she said. "This is restricted parking."

It was just a few minutes before one-thirty and I figured, well, maybe I made a mistake. I drove around the block and I saw two deputies pull into the lot and so I pulled in again.

"You're here again?"

"Yes," I said, "I'm going to bother you one more time."

"Are you here to see a juror?"

"Yes."

"Ah. OK. Pull in over there."

Bureaucracy is a beautiful thing. There was more in store at the door to the building. We're all just standing there outside. A deputy showed up and opened the door, and we went through the routine: name, ID, who we were there to see. Up we went on the elevators to another floor, where we wound around the corner and encountered a group of deputies. Again, name, ID, who we were there to see. Then our things were searched. I was searched and a wand was run over me. My purse was searched. The bag I brought full of things for Tracy was searched.

Finally, I was allowed to go through a door into a big room. Inside were several more deputies patrolling the theater seats and coffee tables and the most elaborate table of food I have ever seen. In fact, it was two long tables, packed with hot food, cold food, fresh fruit, snacks, all of it beautiful, food enough for an army.

As visitors found their jurors, there was a lot of milling about. Visitors exchanged names but the jurors remained numbers.

Tracy and I found a place and sat down. The deputies watched as we went through the mail and we chatted about everyday business. With Tracy unavailable, I'd been forced to take care of all the mundane matters of living. I'm sure the same burden fell on the families of the other jurors. If the refrigerator broke, the dog got sick, or the car needed a muffler, those jobs were all mine. Of course, we were under orders not to talk about the case, but there was no danger of that; we were too busy taking care of family business to devote any time or energy to the case.

Like the night before, I noticed that Tracy seemed unusually animated. That seemed out of character, but I thought it could be explained by any number of different things. Perhaps he was just a bit edgy.

Then I looked carefully into his eyes. We've always communicated with our eyes, always had that special gift.

There was a distance there that I had never before seen.

I started paying close attention to our conversation. We'd be talking about one thing and then, in the middle of something, he would just start talking about something else, as if the first topic had never been broached. If he asked me a question about the new topic, I would answer it and try to direct the conversation back to where it had been. But a few seconds later, he would come back with something else seemingly from left field.

This is the strangest thing, I thought. He's listening to me, but he's not hearing at all. His mind is jumping. He can't sit still. He's either staring straight ahead or looking about furtively. And the case itself hadn't even started yet. Where was this leading?

⋇

The visit the following Sunday brought a vivid demonstration of the tensions that were affecting the jurors' families. As we were waiting outside the Criminal Courts Building, one of the photographers from Camp O.J. came over from across the street and gave us the once-over. Then he approached and said to no one in particular, "Are you here to see someone on the O.J. jury?"

He asked several people, most of whom turned away. When he asked me, I said, "No. I'm here for traffic school."

On a Sunday. It was the best I could think of under the circumstances.

The photographer kept going around, asking questions. Then he took a picture. That did it. One of the family members charged over and yelled at him, told him in no uncertain terms to get lost. The two men almost came to blows.

Just then the deputies opened the door. We went inside and the photographer disappeared.

✛

During the few weeks of waiting around together in lines outside the courthouse door and being shuttled back and forth on Saturday nights to the hotel, we got to know one another, and the conversation inevitably turned to the way the deputies treated us.

The prevailing sense was that the deputies believed us to be a major inconvenience. I'd put my bag up on a table to be searched and was met with a huge sigh from the deputies' side of the table. Never was there eye contact. If one of us would make conversation with them, there rarely was a response. It was not uncommon to hear a family member say, "Why are they treating us like we've done something wrong?"

✛

Though snacks were available at the courthouse, families began bringing food with them. Having worked at Jenny Craig, and being familiar with behavior modification and weight management, I knew that food was a classic mechanism for coping with stress. As the weeks slid by, it became apparent to me what was going on.

Think about it. The jurors sat in court and heard testimony that was unpleasant. They saw gruesome

132

things. They sat so close to the families of the victims that they could physically feel their grief. Yet when the jurors left the box, they were forbidden from talking about it. They had to keep everything inside and make what I call nice-nice with one another. They had to push down this incredible range of feelings.

One of the ways that people cope with anger or rebellion or depression is with food. You feel that feeling, you push it down with food. So jurors were asking their families, "Bring my favorite lemon pie, the one that Mom makes." Or, "Go by El Tepeyac's restaurant and get that burrito I like so much."

It got to the point where we would stand out front by the doors to the Criminal Courts Building and I'd hear the question frequently: "What did you bring for lunch today?" With each week there was more variety and the quantities of food grew larger. Some weeks the quantity was literally staggering. I'd stand there and fret, thinking about all that food and the distance and blankness that I would see in Tracy's eyes. He was not himself, zipping and chattering, his brain wound up a million miles an hour. He'd say something and, zing, there would come something else.

When I'd leave, I wondered if the deputies were noticing what I was picking up in those family visits. The emotional and psychological grind, the predictable responses. To me, red flags were all about. Was anyone else seeing them?

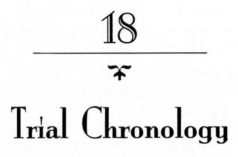

18

Trial Chronology

January 19–January 24, 1995

Thursday
January 19, 1995
9th day of sequestration
Jury not present

• The trial was scheduled to begin today, but due to unfinished business regarding evidence to be included or excluded, opening statements were rescheduled for Monday, January 23, 1995.

• Judge Ito was expected to decide the following day whether the O.J. Simpson defense team can question L.A.P.D. Detective Mark Fuhrman regarding racist statements he is alleged to have made earlier in his career.

• After a closed-door session, attorneys for both sides refused to disclose Judge Ito's plans regarding jury instructions.

Friday
January 20, 1995
10th day of sequestration
Jury not present

• Judge Lance Ito ruled that lawyers for O.J. Simpson will not be permitted to question Detective Mark Fuhrman about racist remarks allegedly made during a workers' compensation case in 1981. Nor will they be allowed to ask questions pertaining to claims that Detective Fuhrman moved or planted evidence in a 1988 officer-involved shooting case.

• Judge Ito said he may allow questions regarding racist remarks allegedly made by Detective Fuhrman as reported by real estate agent Kathleen Bell. The judge withheld a final ruling on that issue.

• Detective Fuhrman, through his attorney, Robert Tourtelot, denied ever having made racist remarks to Kathleen Bell.

• Judge Ito devised a seating chart for the trial,

which was distributed at the end of the day. Each seat is permanently accounted for; nine seats would be open to the public via a daily lottery. A specific number of seats were designated for family members on both sides.

Saturday
January 21, 1995
11th day of sequestration

Sunday
January 22, 1995
12th day of sequestration

Monday
January 23, 1995
13th day of sequestration
Jury not present

• Opening statements, scheduled to start this morning, were again postponed due to motions and evidentiary disputes. At the last minute, defense attorneys presented a list of thirty-four additional witnesses they intend to call.

• Prosecutors accused defense counsel of withholding evidence in order to sabotage the state's case. Although Judge Ito denied a prosecution request for a one-week postponement, he ruled that the defense may not mention twenty-four of the potential witnesses in opening statements, reducing their list to ten.

•   The defense filed an unusual motion allowing the defendant, O.J. Simpson, to give a one-minute statement to the jury, before Johnnie Cochran began his opening remarks. Further, the defense requested that Simpson be allowed to approach the jury box during the defense opening statements to show his scars, injuries, and possible physical limitations.

•   Judge Ito ruled that defense attorneys may cross-examine Detective Mark Fuhrman about his alleged racial slurs against African-Americans. He also ruled that in the opening statements the defense will not be permitted to claim that Fuhrman is a racist who may have planted a bloody glove found at the Simpson Brentwood estate.

•   Opening statements were again rescheduled to begin Tuesday at 10:00 A.M.

Tuesday
January 24, 1995
14th day of sequestration
Jury present

•   Today the long-awaited opening statements began. Christopher Darden was the first prosecutor to address the jury. He was followed by Deputy District

Attorney Marcia Clark. Both outlined what they believe the evidence will show and what they will prove.

• The defense opening statements were delayed when the Court TV camera accidentally showed an eight-tenths-of-a-second flash of an alternate juror who leaned forward into camera range. When informed by Court TV of the error, Judge Ito became irate and threatened to stop televised coverage of the trial. Defense attorneys were rescheduled to begin their opening statements the following morning at ten o'clock.

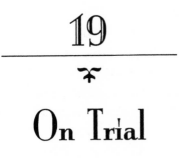

19

On Trial

Tracy

January 24–25, 1995

On Tuesday morning, we were escorted into the jury box. As before, all eyes in the courtroom turned toward the box. Court was finally called back into session. The judge leaned back and said: "Mr. Darden."

With that, the case of The People of the State of California versus Orenthal James Simpson finally got under way. The legal wrangling between the prosecution and the defense which had kept us cooped up in the food room and the hotel for days had mercifully ended. As Christopher Darden rose to speak, the boredom of those days evaporated. I felt a surge of energy. This was it.

I was ready. I'd made up my mind that this was going to be the experience of a lifetime, but I knew I'd have to pay close attention and watch everything in order to absorb everything possible. I planned to enter that jury box each and every day as if my mind was a brand-new sponge, ready to soak up every possible thing: evidence, body language, nuance, words, look, feel. I planned to take copious notes on the steno pad each juror was given. I planned to concentrate even during sidebars. When the judge called the attorneys up to the side of the bench to talk in lowered voices about issues that others, including the jury were not to hear about, I was not going to turn off my mind; instead, I planned to look at the audience, the reporters, or the courtroom, at everything and anything connected to the case. If people thought I was staring, well, that was no concern of mine.

My intent was to make a point of watching O.J. Simpson. I wanted to see his reaction to the evidence as it was presented. All of us know that there's no certain way a guilty person is supposed to look or an innocent person is supposed to act, but I've always been a good judge of body language and trusted my ability to read people. I intended to see what O.J. Simpson's body language told me. I also wanted to watch Judge Ito. I wanted to watch Christopher Darden, Marcia Clark, Robert Shapiro, Johnnie Cochran, F. Lee Bailey, and the others.

I was not particularly interested in watching the

other jurors. I really didn't care what the others thought. Each of us had to bring his or her own opinions and feelings to the table.

It was impossible not to take note of the families of the victims. But after a while, I tried to avoid looking at them. I felt their pain and agony so deeply.

When Darden began speaking that morning, he did so with supreme confidence in his own abilities and in the prosecution's case. In understated tones, he began to lay out the government's case against O.J. Simpson. Marcia Clark followed. She, too, spoke with a forceful assuredness. What they had to say was horrifying. Devastating. Damning.

The prosecutors outlined evidence that seemed overwhelming. It was a double-barreled attack. As Darden talked about why O.J. Simpson did it, Clark explained how it was done.

Jealousy and control, Darden said. The oldest two reasons in the world. That's what did in O.J. Simpson, familiar to all of us as a star athlete, movie star, and TV pitchman.

That public image, Darden said, masked a control freak who tried to dominate his wife. Having failed to control her, Darden continued, O.J. Simpson killed her.

"She left him. She was no longer in his control. He was obsessed with her. He could not stand to lose her. And so he killed her."

Clark devoted her statement to the evidence she said we'd be seeing—blood, hair and fiber evidence that she argued provided physical proof that O.J. Simpson was the killer. She declared that the prosecution would present solid evidence of a "trail of blood" from the victims to the Bronco to O.J.'s own door, even into his bedroom. The blood trail, she said, was "devastating proof" of guilt.

Clark's presentation was powerful. She expressed her firm conviction that the prosecution had the evidence and that they would prove it beyond a reasonable doubt. Looking into her eyes just a few feet away as she set forth the prosecution case hit me hard.

Nothing, however, conveyed the horror of the crime the way the photos did. The prosecution presented photographs of the bloody crime scene—first of Nicole Brown Simpson, then of Ronald Goldman. They were shown on an overhead projector and displayed on a large monitor over the witness stand. Everyone in the courtroom recoiled. Family members sobbed. The gore was tremendous. It was grisly beyond description. I had to force myself to look. Now I can never forget.

One showed a close-up of Nicole Brown Simpson. She was slumped on her side, still dressed in the black halter-top dress she wore to dinner at the Mezzaluna restaurant that night. You could not see the extent of the wounds to her neck, could not tell that her head had very nearly been cut off; her hair hid those facts. But it was no less gruesome, because she was lying in blood that spread out in a pool from her head and trickled down along her body, so much blood that it flowed down the condo walkway.

I looked across the courtroom at O.J. to see his reaction. The light from the overhead projector blocked my view. I couldn't tell if he was looking at the photo or not.

Then came the image of Ron Goldman. His shirt was pulled up. His body was bloody. He had been stabbed repeatedly, and because that shirt was up you could see each of the wounds. They were raw. It looked as if he had put up a fight. He obviously had bled profusely, the loser in ferocious hand-to-hand combat.

The families of the victims sobbed. They were losing their composure and who could blame them? I looked over and the pain in their faces was enormous. I literally felt their grief and thought about how much they would have to endure throughout this trial. I looked again and saw that most of them were crying. The sounds they uttered were those of despair and of a pain that's indescribable. It took a lot of control for me not to cry. This was horror and it was real.

That opening statement left me with a lasting impression. Just as I had suspected when I was first sworn in to the jury, I realized how serious this was and how it would impact me, my family, my future, my job, and everything else that I would look at and deal with for the rest of my life. It wasn't until the two prosecutors laid out their case that I fully understood the horrific nature of the crime. I had never before seen the product of such frenzy and such rage.

Everyone has seen violence like this on TV, but in your mind you say, "Well, it's only a movie." Cutting someone's throat, killing someone, stabbing someone, that's not real, but this was real. There were pictures documenting that it was real. It's incredibly tough to see something like that. It disturbed me deeply that there are actually people in the world who could do that to other human beings. How could that happen? My father had a temper, and I used to watch him explode. And I used to have a temper, but I learned to control it from watching my dad. My father is the reason why I want to be in control of myself, my life, my fate at all times.

Still, all of us have moments where we feel angry and maybe even out of control. But sitting there in that courtroom looking at the picture of two dead people, I could not understand how someone could do that to two fellow beings.

These were two people who were young and who had their whole lives in front of them. They were good-looking. They were vivacious, full of life. And within literally minutes, it was all taken away. They were brutally and senselessly killed.

Seeing those pictures was so unnerving that it became uncomfortable to sit still in the jury box. I made a point of not looking at any of the other jurors, but I think everyone had to be searching his or her soul.

At lunch that day, I did look around at the others. It was awfully quiet in the food room. Of course, we weren't allowed to talk, but it was obvious what was on the mind of each and every person there. As human beings you have to be able to release something that terrible, something you're not used to seeing or experiencing. By not being allowed to talk about it, the emotion builds and builds. Somehow, in some way, it has to come out.

The next day, the defense got its shot. And Johnnie Cochran was magnificent.

He went on so long that he actually did not finish, and he didn't get the chance (for reasons the jury did not know about) for a couple more days. He was silky-smooth. He spoke of Cicero, Abraham Lincoln, and Martin Luther King. He mentioned his mother in Louisiana. He, too, was assured, but he spoke with a casual confidence as he called the prosecution case a "sinister" rush to judgment.

He said that Nicole Brown Simpson had Type B blood under her fingernails. Neither she, Goldman, nor Simpson had that blood type, Cochran said. There were only traces of blood in the white Bronco, far less than expected, Cochran said. Considering Ron Goldman lost so much blood, he added, you'd expect the perpetrator to be drenched in that blood.

Cochran went to great lengths to undercut the prosecution's view of O.J. Simpson as controlling and violent. He portrayed him as a generous man who encouraged Nicole's independence and who gave of himself to her and her family. He called it a "circle of benevolence."

For most of the time that Cochran was speaking, we were looking at an enlarged photograph of O.J. and his daughter, Sydney, taken on the day of the killings. In the photo, O.J. was smiling.

While Cochran spoke, O.J. looked over at us. He lingered in his looks, pausing as he went along, slowly trying to catch the eye of each of the jurors.

Later that afternoon he walked over to the jury box and showed his football scars.

There he was, so close I could touch him. O.J., in the flesh. He lifted his pants to show his knees. He looked awkward, sheepish, and embarrassed.

"These people don't know O.J. Simpson," Cochran said at one point with a dismissive gesture toward the prosecution table. "When you hear about theories, I'm going to tell you about facts."

In a way, Johnnie Cochran had an advantage. He heard what the prosecution had said the day before. He had a whole night to review the way they'd presented their opening statement, and to think about how he could shoot holes in that case. I think he planned it that way. Everyone knows the prosecution has the burden of proving the case beyond a reasonable doubt. I saw that burden as a monumental challenge, like building a pyramid. The prosecution tries to build that pyramid out of nuts and bolts, pieces of sand, gravel, and glass, even toothpicks, anything at all, anything that will hold together. The prosecution hopes that, by the end of the case, the pointy end of that perfect pyramid points directly at the accused. That pyramid has to be just about perfect, too, because the case has to be proven beyond a reasonable doubt. That's a heavy burden. The defense, though, has a different job. It tries to kick little pieces out from the foundation of the pyramid, throw some water on a wall there, dislodge a corner, anything to prevent the construction of that perfect pyramid. The defense doesn't care if the pyramid falls over. They don't care if it points somewhere else. They don't care if there are a lot of points pointing every which way. All they care about is that the pyramid does not point at their client.

The showmanship on both sides was impressive, and I thought to myself, wow, this is going to be a heck of a battle. And that's what it turned out to be. One heck of a battle.

✼

While I was on the phone with Judy, after the prosecution had kicked off the case, I had to remind myself not to say anything. If I needed a powerful reminder, the overseers were standing by, always alert to monitor our calls.

I could tell that night that something was wrong. There was something in her voice.

"The car's OK?"

"Yes."

"Everything OK at work?"

"Oh, yes."

"You're feeling all right?"

"Yes. No problem."

"No headaches. Your migraines aren't acting up?"

"No. I'm fine."

"You're sure everything's OK?"

"Yes, I'm sure. You don't have to worry about anything. I have everything under control."

"Is there something you want to talk about?"

"No. Really. Everything's fine."

But I could tell. It wasn't fine. Something was up.

20

❡

Map People

Judy

January 24, 1995

Late in the afternoon, the phone jangled in my office. "Hello," said a deep voice. "This is Deputy Rufus Downs with the Los Angeles County Sheriff's Department."

"3–21–40," I responded, happy that I knew the code and proud of myself for showing off. That date was my birthday. I'd just identified myself. I decided to show off some more: "I promise I will not talk about the case whatsoever and I know this call may be or is being monitored."

"Ah," said Deputy Downs. "I see you know the

148

magic formula." We both laughed, and he said, "You win the prize."

The prize, I figured, was a conversation with Tracy. As I waited for him to get on the phone, I wondered why the unusual call before seven o'clock in the evening and while I was at work.

Tracy did not get on the phone. Instead, Downs asked, "Have you talked with your husband today?"

"No, I have not."

"My partner and I," Downs said, "have spent all day looking for you. We can't find you."

"Boy, I'm anonymous, aren't I?" The elaborate preparations Tracy and I had undertaken before he'd been sequestered seemed to have paid off. Even a trained investigator couldn't locate me. That was delicious.

"Yes, you really are anonymous," Downs said. "We're at a location now near your house. We need to talk to you before tomorrow morning. We have to ask you some questions that only you can answer."

"Am I in trouble?" A cold shiver of dread raced through me. "Is Tracy all right?"

"We just have some questions that we need to ask that only you can answer."

"I understand. What about tomorrow? It works better for my schedule."

"No. It has to be tonight."

I thought, what could be so urgent? "Well, it's just after five in the afternoon," I said. "It's going to take me an hour to get there from here. It's the height of rush hour."

"That's fine," Downs said. "We'll wait."

"How will I recognize you? Are you in a black and white or are you in an unmarked car? What do you and your partner look like?"

"We're in a pickup truck. And don't worry. You'll know us. We'll introduce ourselves."

"OK," I said. "See you as soon as I can."

The trip home was a never-ending sea of brake lights, stop and go the whole way. I was edgy. The worst thing is always dealing with the unknown. You don't know how to prepare for it emotionally, or what it is you're supposed to prepare for. The whole way home, I worried. A million different scenarios flew through my mind. What could this be about?

A few minutes after I arrived home, the buzzer went off.

"This is Deputy Downs. We're downstairs."

I buzzed them in. I met him and his partner at the elevator. We introduced ourselves. I was so tense I didn't even catch the other deputy's name. We made small talk as we went back down the hall to the condo.

Inside, the small talk ended abruptly. The two deputies pulled out note pads and pens.

"I just need to ask you a few questions," Downs said. "Have you and your husband been out lately?"

"Well," I said, "we went out on New Year's Eve." It was about the only thing we did over the winter holidays.

The pens stayed poised over the notebooks.

"Do you rent a car very often?"

"No."

"Does your husband travel?"

"Yes, he travels."

"Where does he travel?"

I didn't understand where this was leading. "He goes to Oakland," I said. "He goes to Portland. He goes to Seattle. He goes to Salt Lake City. Occasionally, he goes to Beech Grove, Indiana."

"Where is Beech Grove, Indiana, located? Is it near any bigger cities?"

"It's near Indianapolis."

"Is that near Chicago?" People from California. They have no concept of anything east of Las Vegas.

"Yes, it's near Chicago. Indianapolis is just a couple hours away from Chicago on the interstate."

"How does he get to Beech Grove?"

"He takes the train." Naturally. He works for Amtrak. To get to where he wants to go, he takes Amtrak.

"Does he go through Chicago?"

"I'm sure he does. I know that Amtrak does go through Chicago."

"Would he have occasion to rent a car to go from Chicago to Beech Grove?"

"No," I answered. "He takes the train down and then there's an Amtrak van that he has access to."

The pens still had not moved.

"Do you travel?"

"Yes," I said, drawing the word out, as if it were obvious that someone who was an adult and of certain means would travel, either for pleasure or for business. Like to Chicago, as I had just done.

"I went to Chicago the nineteenth and twentieth of this month," I declared.

The pens started scratching across paper. Both men raised their eyebrows.

In that instant, I made the connection, and I slammed my hand on the table in disbelief at how I'd been so dense. I'd blithely missed what suddenly seemed so obvious. Chicago. That's where O.J. Simpson had gone on the red-eye just hours after Nicole Brown Simpson and Ronald Goldman had been killed. And I'd taken Tracy a map of Chicago.

"The nineteenth and twentieth?" Downs asked.

"Yes."

"Where did you stay?"

I told them.

"Did you rent a car?"

"No."

"How did you get to the hotel?"

"I took one of those ride-share limos."

"What was the nature of this trip? Pleasure or business?"

"Business. The office I went to was about two blocks from the hotel. In fact," I said, "I got a map of Chicago in the room, and I took it to my husband to show him where I stayed, where the office I'd gone to was located. I also showed him the places I'd gone to eat."

Now the pens were going furiously.

"Would there be any reason to have a map of Los Angeles?"

"Well, I just picked that up," I said. "Look over here." I pointed to a stand nearby where there was a South Coast Air Quality Management District map showing air flow and smog patterns in the Los

152

Angeles basin. In a pile by the table, underneath the kitchen counter, were more maps. There were a couple of fold-out American Automobile Association (AAA) maps of California and a variety of other road maps of different places. "I was in a hurry to get to see Tracy on Saturday. I'd just gotten back from Chicago that afternoon, I was racing around the condo, and I picked up the map on the spur of the moment because I thought it would be interesting. We're map people. In fact, in his study we have three large maps."

"Do you mind if we see them?"

"Not at all."

We trooped into the study. There on the wall were the three raised relief maps of the United States, California, and Los Angeles.

"Well," Downs said as we walked back to the living room, "you really are map people."

"We really are. Tracy and I share things, we like to share things, and there were things on that trip to Chicago that I wanted to share with him."

Both deputies wrote for a bit, then sat quietly for a bit more, thinking about where to take the conversation next.

"Do you have your ticket?" Downs asked.

"My airplane ticket?"

"Yes."

"Yes, I do."

"May I have it, please?"

"Um," I said, thinking about it, "sure." Why not?

"Your hotel bill, too. That will include the phone calls you made, I assume. If you made phone calls on a charge card and you have that bill, I'd appreciate that, too."

"OK, sure." Suddenly deciding that I really ought to be helpful, I told him about my daily schedule in Chicago. While I talked I fished out a collection of tickets and receipts. I even mentioned what time I had used the exercise room each night at the hotel. I told him about what I'd eaten, and the colleagues I'd eaten with. I added, however, that we had walked to the restaurant, so I did not have a receipt for cab fare.

I handled this jumbled mess of papers to Downs.

"It's OK if I take this?" he asked.

"Yes."

Downs looked me in the eyes. "Have you talked today to your husband?"

"No."

"Would you please not mention this to your husband?"

"Fine."

About a half-hour after the deputies left, Tracy called. He knew I had something to tell him. I knew he knew. But I couldn't say a word.

Something was up. He could just tell.

The next morning, one of the Los Angeles newspapers reported that authorities were investigating one of the jurors in the O.J. Simpson double-murder trial because maps of Chicago were found in that juror's room. The juror's identity was not mentioned. Authorities, the newspaper story said, were concerned that the juror might be conducting his own investigation into the circumstances surrounding O.J. Simpson's June 12 flight to Chicago.

As I read the story, it seemed that every drop of blood drained out of my body. My fingers and toes tingled. I felt woozy.

I was crushed. To think that there was an investigation into something that seemed so innocent, and that my husband was the one suspected of wrongdoing. And, worst of all, that I was the cause of it all.

21

Investigation

Tracy

Late January 1995

The few times I'd been in Judge Ito's chambers, the mood was always light, the conversation cheery, the judge solicitous.

So when I was summoned to chambers by the judge's clerk, Deirdre Robertson, I thought nothing of it. I put on a big smile, entered the room, and said, "Hi. How is everyone?"

Ten, maybe fifteen people were crowded into the room. There was the judge. Around the room were the famous and familiar faces of the lawyers: Marcia Clark, Christopher Darden, Robert Shapiro, Johnnie

Cochran. Near the judge were a couple of security types; they were big and burly.

Judge Ito was sitting behind his desk, an old, dark, solid block of wood. It was impressive and he looked formidable behind it. He was framed by row upon row of law books. He was in shirt sleeves, his robe hanging on a clothes tree behind his desk, reserved for appearances in court. Even without it, he looked as if he was taking the measure of me. The lawyers were arranged so that each attorney could get a good look at me.

Everyone was dead serious. I couldn't figure out what was wrong. The air in there abruptly seemed dense, hard to breathe.

"It has been reported to me," Judge Ito said, "that you have a map of Chicago."

The stenographer went clickety-clack on her machine. Although a transcript would tell you this word for word, I think I said something like, "Yes, that's true. It is on my desk."

"Yes, I know," he responded. Then he asked sharply, "What were you doing with a map of Chicago in your hotel room?"

"My wife brought it and we were discussing her trip to Chicago. She made a trip to Chicago on business. It was her first time there. I told her some sights she ought to see. She told me where she went, what she saw, what she did, where the office was that she was working out of."

I still had no feel for the gravity of the situation. Everyone else in the room looked intent and so incredibly serious.

"Do you realize Chicago has a bearing on this case?" Judge Ito asked.

Oh.

Now I understood. O.J. had gone to Chicago on the red-eye.

"I hadn't even thought of that," I told the judge. "I really didn't think of that."

"Occasionally," Judge Ito said, "we get jurors in the system who want to do investigations on their own into the evidence they hear in court. That is improper."

I said nothing. I thought to myself, how in the world would I be able to investigate anything? I'm sequestered.

"You had another map," Judge Ito said. This was as much a question as a statement.

"I did?"

"What were you doing with a map of Los Angeles?"

"Well," I said, "I don't really know why my wife brought that map of L.A. If I had to guess, it would be that it was just with the maps we have in a pile underneath our kitchen counter and she just picked it up as she was leaving the house. But I don't know."

"What did you do with the map?"

"I showed her where we had gone on one of our outings. I told her the outing not connected with the case, had been nice and that we ought to go there and visit ourselves."

"Are you certain that's all that you were using this map for?"

"Yes. Why?"

"We're not allowed to have any private investigations by a juror."

"I understand. Should I throw the maps away?"

"I've got them now," he said. "I'll keep them."

The judge said that the matter would be investigated further. He wasn't sure how long that investigation would take. "All right," he said. "You may go back to the jury room. Do not speak with any of the other members of the jury about what we have discussed in here."

I left the judge's chambers and turned toward the jury room. I'm not quite certain how my feet knew to keep going. I was in a fog.

When I got back into the room, I felt a pressing need to sit down. Standing up seemed a physical impossibility. It was too much work while I was so consumed with thought. I simply had to sit down.

My face was white as a sheet. No one said a word to me.

Fifteen or twenty minutes later, we were called into the courtroom. We filed in just like any other day except for me. I was dumbfounded. I tried to piece together the chain of events that had led the judge to summon me. Someone had been in my room and seen the maps. Well, they were in plain view, they weren't hard to find. Supposedly, the only ones who had access to our rooms were the hotel maids and the overseers. Supposedly, an overseer was assigned to keep watch over the maid while she was straightening up. So an overseer had to have snapped up the maps. That made no sense. But neither did this entire episode. Some overseer obviously had to look at and approve the maps when Judy presented her things for the Saturday night search. Someone with a badge and a gun searched her bag that night and clearly had to have seen the maps and just as clearly put them back in the bag.

In the light of day, apparently, the maps looked far more sinister to the sheriff's department.

The rules were so clear, so well defined, or so the overseers would have you believe. And now I was in hot water for something I didn't even know I was doing wrong.

One thing was clear. I had no privacy. Perhaps, I thought, the overseers had really been planning to plant bugs in my room and stumbled upon the maps. Perhaps they had been planning to install more bugs, on top of the ones that surely had to be in the room, seeking to enhance their already formidable listening capacity.

Maybe now I was marked as a troublemaker who deserved extra scrutiny. Maybe I'd earned a little special attention from the sheriff's department.

I'd have to give the room a thorough go-through. I'd have to resort to one of those tricks you see in spy movies like putting a thread or a piece of paper somewhere so that I would know if it had been disturbed. If the room was being searched regularly while I was in court, I wanted to know. I vowed to take up all the secret agent tricks I could think of.

My mind was really wandering. I was nearly twitching from the rush of paranoia. I fought it back, blinked my eyes, shook my head, and focused on the back and forth of the testimony in the courtroom.

✴

That night, as I was walking past the Control Point in the hotel hallway, I overheard one of the overseers whispering to a colleague.

"He's the one with the maps," she said, embellishing the remark with a knowing nod in my direction.

I thought long and hard about what she said, and whether she intended to intimidate me. I couldn't decide.

✴

For a week or more, I was left hanging. No one said a thing to me about the maps.

Judy arrived for a conjugal visit and we finally talked about it together. We knew we hadn't done anything wrong *intentionally* and we were happy when they found us innocent, or so we thought.

It was several weeks, however, before I got to see Judge Ito again. He was back to his solicitous self. We talked a bit about me wanting to exercise in the morning. Of course, I had written him a note about that.

"Before we chat about that," he said, "let me just tell you, to put your mind at ease. I don't know if I did this appropriately, but after our map incident, we did, you know, conduct our investigation, found the explanation to be as you said, and completely benign, so I mean the reason you are still here is because are you are [*sic.*] still here."

"I was hoping that was the reason," I said.

"You have to understand that it did immediately cause us some concern," continued the judge. "Because of the connection between Chicago and Los Angeles, and you are probably not aware of this, but in many, many other cases we have had problems with juries where they have gone out and gotten maps to equate distances and determine travel times and that sort of thing when it is important to the case, so that is why maps are immediately suspicious when we see one of those.

"But your explanation was completely benign and completely believable, and after we corroborated everything, that is closed, as far as that is concerned."

"Thank you," I said.

So I was in the clear. But the damage had already been done. I started searching the room regularly for bugs.

Nothing ever turned up.

I also began leaving a thread in a groove on one of my suitcases, underneath some shoes. When I came back to the room each afternoon, I checked the thread to make sure it was still there. One day, the thread was missing. I checked my clothes; everything was there but moved all around. I checked my things; they were all there.

I suspected everyone. I could not rule out any possibilities.

22

Feeling the Pressure

Judy

February 1995

Waiting is always the hardest part. It took a week and a half for Deputy Downs to tell me that Tracy had been cleared.

It was ten days of near-constant anguish.

The papers were full of stories about this investigation. My stomach churned at each headline. As I scanned each story, I'd either tense up or relax, depending on the tone. Then I'd think about these stories all day long. I'd think to myself, I can't do this, I have to concentrate at work. I can't be addicted to this cycle, I have to let go of this. Just be patient, I'd tell myself, it will be fine. Be calm.

That would settle me down for a moment. Then my mind would switch back to overdrive, and I would find myself bedeviled by a stream of questions to which I had no answers: Is someone searching Tracy's room? How is he holding up?

There finally came a point where I couldn't stand it anymore. I heard yet another breathless report on the TV news about an investigation into a juror, something to do with maps, so I lunged for the telephone. I called the number Deputy Downs had given me. I was in tears and ended up speaking first with a sheriff's lieutenant. "There was nothing wrong," I wailed into the phone. "I gave all this information to Deputy Downs." I was nearly hysterical.

The lieutenant put Downs on the phone. "I want you to know," Downs said, "that I just talked with the judge this morning and we realize it was an innocent thing. Don't worry about it."

I was both relieved and furious and all this pent-up emotion came spilling out.

"Let me tell you something," I said to Downs. "You asked me not to say anything to anyone about this. So if only you and I and the judge knew about this, how did it get into the paper? You have a serious leak somewhere." I didn't understand then that the lawyers in the case, as well as court clerks and other sheriff's deputies, also knew about the maps. All I knew is that I'd been told to keep quiet, and I had obeyed that directive.

I was also just warming up. "As long as we're talking," I said, "I need to tell you that it would be advantageous if you would have a crisis intervention team come talk with these jurors. I'm beginning to notice some things about my husband that concern me a great deal." I told Deputy Downs that I felt I was losing my husband visually and that Tracy was turning inward. I also told the deputy, in elaborate detail, about the mountains of food that were being brought to Sunday family visits, and the connection between that food and stress. Finally I suggested that psychological specialists visiting the jurors could have real benefits.

Downs told me he thought it was a good idea and he'd mention it to someone.

The stress of sequestration was hitting the other families, too. They did not have the added burden of an investigation but nonetheless were definitely feeling the pressure.

Tentatively, we began to talk to one another on those Saturday night van rides to the hotel. Starsky and Hutch paid us no mind.

"I feel as if I'm losing communication with him," one family member said.

"She just sits there each Sunday," said another. "There's such a blank look on her face."

"It's getting bad," said a third.

"Something really ought to be done," someone said. "It's as if they're hostages and we're the ones left at home, tying yellow ribbons around a tree."

In the dark van, the conversation kept going. I floated the idea of a seminar on stress management, put on for our benefit by the sheriff's department or the courts. The others thought that was a great idea and soon we were eagerly discussing the different possibilities. Everyone felt the need to talk with stress counselors, psychologists, or other mental health professionals who could educate us about forced separation and the range of feelings we were likely to experience. Maybe they could reassure us that feeling paranoid and edgy was, in all likelihood, perfectly normal.

If we could have known that what the jurors were feeling was normal, it would have been wonderfully reassuring. Just to be told that it was normal for us, on the outside, to feel that way, too, would have been a blessing. But the psychological and emotional strain on the families of the jurors was not discussed. When I talked to Tracy I always felt enormous pressure to be up, perky almost, because I didn't want him worrying about me.

Over the week, I thought of other ideas that seemed reasonable. Simple steps for mental health like giving the jurors notebooks like the one I gave Tracy so they could have an outlet for their feelings, and organizing sessions where the families could write out their feelings, too. The jurors could fill out periodic evaluations about their living conditions. Families could be asked to make their visits better. Each one of these ideas could have been accomplished without disclosing anyone's name or invading anyone's privacy.

The following Saturday someone came up to me before we got in the van and said, "I just want you to know that your idea of a seminar is really great. I thought about it all week, and I hope you actually do something about making it happen."

That was a good push. At the beginning of the following week, I called the sheriff's department and pointed out the benefits of a stress management seminar. "Something really needs to be done," I said to one of the deputies. "The fallout from this is reaching significant levels. We're all beginning to feel it. We know the jurors are feeling it because we're seeing this blankness in their faces."

"Are we having a problem with a specific juror?" the deputy asked. "If you tell me the number, I'll be sure to have someone look into it promptly."

"No!" I cried into the phone in frustration. "That's not the point. We're not having a problem with any one particular juror. I just think it would be an excellent idea if your department brought in someone to talk to the jurors, and brought in someone separately to talk to the families, about the stresses of being sequestered. That's all I'm saying."

There was silence for a moment at the other end of the phone. Then the deputy said, "Sounds like a good idea."

I never heard another word from the sheriff's department about it.

One Sunday, on my way to Family Visit, I stopped by the grocery store. After I got what I needed, I came out and discovered I had locked the keys in the car.

Panicky thoughts ripped through my mind: If I wasn't in the line at one-thirty that afternoon, the deputies wouldn't let me into the courthouse. No way to call. Can't be late. What to do?

It was hot. I couldn't think straight. I was in Tracy's car. I tried the trunk, hoping it was open. No. I tried the other doors. Everything was locked.

I ran back into the store and begged for a coat hanger. Luckily, someone had one. I ran back outside, jammed the coat hanger down the door, slid it up and down. Nothing. Where's the lock? How does the stupid thing work? How long would it take for AAA to get here? How does this trick with the hangers work?

A stockboy came out. "Ma'am, can I give you a hand?"

"Oh, yes, please. Please. Can you make this work? I'd be so grateful. I can't even tell you how appreciative I'd be. I have got to get to the Criminal Courts Building. That's downtown. I've just got to get there." I rattled on. I was hyper. My heart was pounding. I felt warm. Got to get there. Think, think, think.

The emergency number. I went to the phone and dialed 411. Maybe I could get the emergency number from information.

This was not a true emergency, I knew, as I rehearsed what I would say: I'm sorry I used this number, I locked my keys in the car, please understand the situation, I was still planning to be there, just please let me in when I arrive, let Tracy know I am all right.

At the time, it seemed like the most important thing in the entire universe. The operator gave me a number for the Criminal Courts Building, and I dialed it and someone answered. Yes! I poured out my entire story, just as I'd rehearsed it.

"Ah, ma'am," came the voice at the other end of the phone, "it's Sunday. The Criminal Courts Building is closed."

"Is this the emergency number for the O.J. Simpson jury?"

"Ah, no, ma'am, it is not."

"Who is this?"

"I'm just the operator, ma'am. The building is closed."

I began to tell her how important my situation was, and I asked her to tell someone, anyone, that I was on my way to see my husband. I hung up. I fished around in my purse for quarters and called AAA and they said they were on their way.

At that moment, the stockboy walked up with the keys. I started to sob.

I cried uncontrollable tears. I'm not a hysterical person, but right then and there I felt so much pressure I was hysterical. Huge, salty tears rolled down my cheeks.

The stockboy was alarmed. "Ma'am, are you OK?"

"Thank you, thank you, thank you," I told him as I grabbed the keys and threw myself into the car.

When I got to the courthouse, I was ten minutes late. Still feeling rattled, I told a deputy at the door my entire story. I told him how I had to find the emergency number but didn't know what it was and couldn't get it from the 411 operator.

"In the future, do not use that number if you have locked your keys in the car, ma'am," the deputy said.

It felt as if he had poured ice water on me. I tried to explain, but the deputy shot me a look that said, you were doubly stupid. You locked your keys in the car. And then you violated protocol by thinking that you were entitled to dial the emergency number.

When I finally got upstairs, I saw Tracy sitting on a little box inside this big room with a look on his face that suggested he was all alone in the world. He looked so small, like a child who had been left alone at the mall and didn't know who to call or how to get home. He looked so lost.

When Tracy saw me, I could tell he'd been worried. I was always one of the first through the door. He was worried, then angry, then irritated. I was irritated at myself, too, and irritated at him for being upset with me. But by then we were so practiced at not showing each other what was really going on inside our minds that we didn't dare risk talking about it.

Each week the division between us grew wider and wider. Each week, Tracy became more and more animated while discussing the movies he'd seen. When he talked about films that were violent, I noticed he'd become hostile. It seemed so obvious to me that he was trying to play out the feelings and emotions that were raging inside him, and was using the medium of the movie to express himself.

It was as if Tracy was on Planet O.J. during the week, and then for a few hours each Sunday he was jerked back to some semblance of the real world. But as the trial wore on, the Tracy I saw was not the same. With each week, more and more of his humanity seemed to be missing. His eyes would dart about the room, fixing only briefly on me before setting off again around the room, as if he were a combat pilot scanning each of his instruments in a fast and furious rotation. He was withdrawn and he was overly suspicious. I wondered, what happened to my Tracy? And what was happening to me?

23

✶

Trial Chronology

January 25–February 12, 1995

Wednesday
January 25, 1995
15th day of sequestration
Jury present

• Judge Lance Ito declared that the Court TV camera could remain in the courtroom as long as steps were taken to ensure that no jurors would be televised.

• Johnnie Cochran, Jr., began the opening statements for the defense. He said O.J. Simpson is "an

172

innocent man wrongly accused." Cochran character-
ized the police investigation as sloppy, suggesting
that much of the prosecution evidence was tainted
and that the investigation against O.J. was a "rush to
judgment."

- O.J. Simpson became a living exhibit at his trial
for the double homicide of Nicole Brown Simpson
and Ronald Goldman. He was permitted to show the
jurors the football injuries to his knees, and also to
display his hands.

Jury not in court

- Out of the jury's presence, Deputy District Attorney William Hodgman angrily accused the defense
team of violating discovery rules by failing to turn
over witnesses' names before opening statements. An
irate Hodgman vigorously urged Judge Ito to sanction defense counsel for misconduct that he contends
has severely prejudiced the prosecution's case.

Our of court

- At a late meeting of the prosecution team in the
District Attorney's office, William Hodgman was
stricken with chest pains and transported to a local
hospital.

Thursday
January 26, 1995
16th day of sequestration
Jury not present

• Judge Ito canceled the regular session of the trial for January 26 and 27.

• The court was occupied by a day-long hearing regarding possible sanctions against the defense for failure to turn over witness statements and other items to the prosecution in a timely manner, as required by the rules of discovery.

• Prosecutors accused the defense of referring to the expected testimony of defense witnesses in their opening statements, when the prosecutors had not been given those witness statements. The prosecutors suggested a thirty-day continuance and the opportunity to give additional opening statements as appropriate sanctions.

• Prosecutor Christopher Darden denounced the proposed defense witnesses as "heroin addicts, thieves, felons, and . . . the only person I have ever known to be a court-certified pathological liar." He stated that prospective defense witness Mary Ann Gerchas owed $23,000 to the J. W. Marriott Corp. "We know she had nine lawsuits pending in the D.A.'s office. In our bad check section there are approximately $10,000 in bad checks that relate to this person," Darden said.

• The session was filled with heated exchanges between the judge and the attorneys for both sides as all the participants' patience appeared to be wearing thin.

Outside of court

• William Hodgman, hospitalized last night after suffering chest pains, remained in the hospital under observation.

Friday
January 27, 1995
17th day of sequestration
Jury not present

• The battle over the defense's failure to turn over discovery escalated in front of Judge Ito. Both sides presented their recommendations as to possible sanctions the judge might impose. Acrimonious debate marked the session, in which Judge Ito did not issue a ruling.

• Following the judge's ruling on the request for a delay by the prosecution, the defense is expected to continue opening statements—which were halted earlier in the week—when the trial resumes on Monday morning.

Outside of court

• William Hodgman was released from the hospital and was resting at home.

Saturday
January 28, 1995
18th day of sequestration

Sunday
January 29, 1995
19th day of sequestration

Monday
January 30, 1995
20th day of sequestration
Jury present

• The trial resumed for the first time since last Wednesday when opening statements by Johnnie Cochran were brought to a halt over the defense's failure to provide discovery.

• Judge Lance Ito ruled that as a sanction to the defense for failure to comply with the rules of discovery, the prosecution would be given the opportunity to make additional opening statements. He further instructed the jurors that Johnnie Cochran had violated the law when he failed to provide the prosecution with the witness statements. The jurors were asked to disregard Cochran's remarks from last Wednesday about witnesses who had been concealed by the defense to obtain an unfair tactical advantage over the prosecution.

• Johnnie Cochran concluded his opening remarks by criticizing the quality of the prosecution evidence gathering as careless and slipshod, resulting in contamination.

176

Tuesday
January 31, 1995
21st day of sequestration
Jury present

• In an unusual ruling by Judge Lance Ito, prosecutor Marcia Clark was granted ten minutes to reopen her opening statements. She assailed prospective defense witness Mary Anne Gerchas as a "known liar" and a "Simpson case groupie."

• The prosecution opened with testimony from witnesses detailing a 1989 spousal battery call at the O.J. Simpson Brentwood estate. Sharyn Gilbert, the 911 operator, Detective Mike Farrell, and Detective John Edwards testified.

Outside the courtroom

• A bomb scare outside the courthouse involving a newspaper rack containing what appeared to be a pipe bomb resulted in police detonating the device. It was not a bomb. The building was not cleared, but the immediate area in front of the courthouse was.

Wednesday
February 1, 1995
22nd day of sequestration
Jury present

• Judge Lance Ito, after hearing arguments from both sides regarding the admissibility of proposed testimony by witness Ronald Shipp, ruled for the prosecution. Ronald Shipp took the stand.

• Shipp was questioned by Christopher Darden for the prosecution. Carl Douglas for the defense conducted the cross-examination.

• Court was recessed early to allow members of the O.J. Simpson defense team to attend the funeral of Simpson's friend Bob Chandler. Chandler was a former football player who died of lung cancer the previous Friday.

Thursday
February 2, 1995
23rd day of sequestration
Jury present

• Ron Shipp continued on the stand, cross-examined by Carl Douglas for the defense. Douglas toned down his previously abrasive demeanor on cross.

• Michael Stevens, the senior District Attorney, investigator who opened the safe deposit box of Nicole Brown Simpson to reveal photos of her with bruises, took the stand for the prosecution. Also in the safe were other items, including a handwritten letter of apology from O.J. Simpson.

• Tape of an October 25, 1993, call to 911 was played. Witness Terri Moore, the 911 operator, testified she had received the call, which emanated from the residence of Nicole Simpson.

• Robert Lerner, the officer who came to the Gretna Green house in response to Nicole Simpson's 911 call, testified for the prosecution.

Outside of court

• Judge Ito met with Los Angeles County Sheriff's deputies who were part of an investigation into possible misconduct of jury members.

Friday
February 3, 1995
24th day of sequestration
Jury present

• Neighbor Catherine Boe, who lived next door to Nicole Simpson on Gretna Green in 1992 and whose son was a friend of Justin Simpson, testified for the prosecution about domestic incidents to which she was a witness.

• Carl Colby, Boe's husband, testified to seeing someone looking at Nicole Simpson's house late at night. He called 911 thinking it was a burglar. It turned out to be O.J. Simpson.

• Denise Brown, look-alike sister of the deceased Nicole Simpson, testified to incidents of physical abuse by O.J. Simpson. She testified for approximately twenty minutes before breaking down. Prosecutor Darden asked that Miss Brown be excused until Monday, as it was only ten minutes until the designated 3:00 P.M. end of the session.

Jury not present

• Deputy District Attorney Rockne Harmon, a prosecution DNA expert, challenged remarks from Johnnie Cochran's opening statement regarding blood evidence on a pair of socks found in O.J. Simpson's bedroom.

• Robert Blasier, a DNA expert for the defense, disagreed with prosecution allegations. Judge Ito asked for information on the blood testing for Monday.

Saturday
February 4, 1995
25th day of sequestration

Sunday
February 5, 1995
26th day of sequestration

Monday
February 6, 1995
27th day of sequestration
Jury present

• Denise Brown, sister of Nicole Brown Simpson, concluded her testimony for the prosecution. She was cross-examined by Robert Shapiro for the defense.

• Candace Garvey, wife of former baseball player Steve Garvey, and a friend of Nicole Simpson, was the next witness. She testified for the prosecution about O.J. Simpson's behavior at Sydney Simpson's dance recital.

• Cynthia Shahian, jogging partner and friend of Nicole Simpson, testified about a letter O.J. Simpson sent Nicole Simpson in June regarding the Internal Revenue Service.

Tuesday
February 7, 1995
28th day of sequestration
Jury present

• Another juror was removed by Judge Lance Ito. A sixty-three-year-old retired legal secretary was replaced by a fifty-four-year-old postal worker.

• Stewart Tanner, a bartender at Mezzaluna, the restaurant where Ronald Goldman worked, testified for the prosecution about the last known activities of the deceased.

- Pablo Fenjves, a neighbor of Nicole Simpson, testified to hearing a dog's wailing between 10:15 and 10:20 P.M. the night of the killings.

- Kimberly Goldman, sister of Ron Goldman, testified briefly, identifying the work clothes found in her brother's apartment after his death.

- Tia Gavin and Karen Crawford, Mezzaluna employees, described the last time they saw Ron Goldman.

    Jury not present

- Defense attorney Johnnie Cochran complained about the small angel pin that Marcia Clark was wearing. Judge Ito reserved judgment until the following day.

    Wednesday
    February 8, 1995
    29th day of sequestration
    Jury present

- Eva Stein, a neighbor of Nicole Simpson on Bundy, testified as to the time (10:15 P.M.) she was awakened by loud barking.

- Louis Karpf, Eva Stein's fiancé, testified that he returned from a trip and was outside getting his mail at 11:00 P.M. when he was frightened by Kato the dog and went back inside.

• Steven Schwab testified he was walking his dog in the neighborhood when he saw an Akita with bloody paws. He took the dog to his apartment. His neighbor agreed to watch the dog until they could locate the owner.

• Sukru Boztepe, Schwab's neighbor, testified that he and his wife walked the dog, and it led them to discover the body of Nicole Brown Simpson. He called 911.

• Elsie Tistaert, an elderly lady who lived nearby, testified that she heard a dog barking for about thirty minutes. Around midnight she called 911 when she thought she heard prowlers, at about the time Mr. Boztepe and his wife were attempting to find a telephone and had knocked on Ms. Tistaert's door.

Jury not present

• Judge Ito declined to squash the subpoena for Marguerite Simpson Thomas, first wife of O.J. Simpson. Mrs. Thomas claimed through her attorney, Carl Jones, that the document was served illegally. Judge Ito ruled that her testimony is relevant regarding two telephone calls she received from O.J. Simpson June 13 prior to his arrest.

• Announced defense witness Mary Anne Gerchas was booked in West Los Angeles on felony grand theft and fraud charges.

• Judge Ito determined that it was inappropriate for Marcia Clark to wear her angel pin.

Thursday
February 9, 1995
30th day of sequestration
Jury present

• Pictures of the crime scene were revealed in court as L.A.P.D. Officer Robert Riske, first officer on the scene, described what he saw. Mr. and Mrs. Brown, parents of slain Nicole Brown Simpson, exited the courtroom before the photos were shown. Mrs. Goldman and Kim Goldman remained in court, with Kim crying quietly. Marcia Clark conducted the questioning of Robert Riske, the only witness of the day.

• Judge Ito told the jurors that they would be going on a field trip to Brentwood in the near future to view pertinent locations.

Jury not present

• William Hodgman, an original prosecutor in the O.J. Simpson trial, returned to work today as case manager. He will perform this function outside the courtroom.

• Defense witness Mary Anne Gerchas was arraigned in West Los Angeles before Judge George H. Wu. She pleaded not guilty to felony fraud charges of defrauding an innkeeper when she failed to pay a hotel bill for $23,000. She was released on $20,000 bail.

Friday
February 10, 1995
31st day of sequestration
Court not in session.

• Today Judge Lance Ito led lawyers from both sides on a preview tour of the Brentwood area in preparation for the jury tour. The official jury tour is scheduled to take place on Sunday.

Saturday
February 11, 1995
32nd day of sequestration

Sunday
February 12, 1995
33rd day of sequestration

• The jury field trip took place.

24
❦

Photos and a Field Trip

Tracy

February 1995

In court, the pace of the trial finally picked up. We listened to 911 calls and to testimony about everything from O.J. Simpson's dreams to barking dogs. I tried to soak it all up. I kept telling myself, be like a sponge.

Denise Brown, Nicole's sister, took the stand. She looked like Nicole but with black hair. Eerie.

It really was very strange. There was Denise, living, breathing, grieving, right there on the witness stand just a few feet away. But Nicole was dead. The only images of her that lingered were the ones in the crime scene photos. There she was in that black cocktail dress, as if she were asleep. You could almost believe that was the case. Except for the pool of blood flowing from Nicole's body down to the sidewalk. Or the one picture in which her blonde hair was soaked in blood.

The photos were shown again in court, projected on the screen above the witness box. It was easy to tell when there would be an especially gory shot on the screen. Apparently, Judge Ito had ordered that the stomach-wrenching gore not be shown on television, so every time someone said, "Cut the feed," I knew that the picture coming right up was going to be horrible.

Indeed, they were. They were so bloody, so devastating, that no words could do them justice.

They were so bad that the Brown family got up and left the courtroom. The Goldmans stayed, but Kim Goldman cried softly. I tried desperately not to look at the families, but it was impossible not to hear the sobs in the still courtroom. The tension in the court was palpable.

I made a point of not looking at the others in the jury box. Instead, I focused my attention on O.J.; I was most interested in what his reaction would be.

He made a point of not looking at any of the photos. I watched him closely. With each picture, he looked away. Even for photos of Ron Goldman, he turned his head away from the image on the screen.

What, I wondered, was going on in O.J.'s mind as the slides flashed on the screen?

That day in court, Judge Ito announced that he

was planning to take us on a field trip to Brentwood to see the sites we were seeing in the photos. When the lawyers talked about *Rockingham* or *Bundy* or used an even more specific term, such as *behind Kato's room*, we'd all have the same specific picture in our minds.

Beyond that, of course, was the realization that we'd actually see real life again. There would be streets and people and signs. Maybe even some sunshine.

It's important to stress that none of us on the jury viewed the field trip as a lark in the park. This was serious business. But after a month in confinement, the idea of fresh sights was a welcome proposition.

"I'll see you when I see you," Judge Ito said that Thursday in court.

On Saturday evening, the night before our trip, we were assembled and read the ground rules for the trip. More rules.

"These rules will be strictly enforced," an overseer said. "Do not talk to anyone while viewing the crime scene. I repeat, do not . . ."

It was suggested that we dress casually. The forecast was for rain. I opted the next morning for jeans, the one and only time I wore blue jeans, and a sportcoat.

We marched in our lines down to the hotel parking garage and rode over to the courthouse. The usual routine, except this time we didn't get out of the vans. Instead, we waited in the garage of the court-house. "What's going on?" people started grumbling.

Because we'd been living in isolation, we had no idea of the complete circus the case had become. We had long before accepted that there was intense public attention focused on the trial. That's why there were so many reporters in the audience each day, why there was a live TV feed, and why our newspapers were in such tatters. But we had no appreciation for the frenzy the case had generated since the trial itself had begun. Killing time there in that garage, we had no idea of the lengths to which Judge Ito had gone to protect our identities and our security that day. He apparently wanted something extraordinary. And, as we were about to learn, that's what he got.

"Let's go!" came the order over the radio.

I saw a bus with the windows completely tinted so that you couldn't see in. We were ordered to get on the bus. On board, it was clear that this was a bus designed to carry prisoners. Inside was a cage for unruly inmates and bars over the windows. We each found a seat.

Someone told us where we were headed. First, where Ron Goldman lived. Then by Mezzaluna, the restaurant where he worked, the last place anyone had seen him or Nicole Brown Simpson alive. Then to Nicole's condominium on Bundy Drive. Then to O.J. Simpson's mansion on Rockingham Avenue.

"There is to be no talking," we were reminded. "Do not speak among yourselves. Do not speak to the deputies. This rule will be strictly enforced."

The bus pulled out of the garage under the courthouse. I could not believe what I was seeing.

We were in a caravan that included police on motorcycles as well as unmarked police cars and vans. Surrounding us was a virtual army of police officers, sheriff's deputies, and marshals. There were scores of news crews. Overhead came the rhythmic *wock-wock-wock* of helicopters. I counted a half-dozen before I stopped counting. I didn't know it at the time, but Judge Ito had even blocked off the airspace above us. Amazing.

It was more elaborate than any presidential motorcade I had seen. It truly was beyond belief. Each intersection had been blocked off to prevent any access to the bus, and police officers manned each intersection. Actually, there were police officers everywhere, it seemed. They were like fleas on a dog, they were so thick along the route.

As we roared out toward upscale Brentwood, the helicopters buzzed along with us. Some were police helicopters, but others were TV choppers. Live and in living color—the O.J. jury roadshow!

The most amazing thing of all, however, was that there was no traffic on Interstate 10, the Santa Monica Freeway. An L.A. freeway without any other motor vehicles on it. Just our caravan. Incredible. That is a testament to Judge Ito's power. We roared down the Santa Monica Freeway and I remember thinking how funny it had been that the driver of the bus had told us as we'd boarded not to worry, that he was a good driver. What was to worry? A traffic school loser could have driven the freeway that morning without incident.

As we left the freeway and neared Brentwood, the crowds grew thicker and thicker along the side of the streets. It was like being in a parade where we were the grand marshals. Cars honked. People waved.

Inside the bus, no one waved back.

This is how it was all the way to Ron Goldman's apartment. We paused there, then lumbered over to Mezzaluna. The restaurant was closed for the morning. I took in the entire neighborhood. Across the street was the Ben and Jerry's ice cream store. In that same strip mall was a bookstore. Across another street was a grocery store. I looked at the faces in the throng, all the people watching us, and wondered how many of the people there were friends or acquaintances of Ron Goldman or Nicole Brown Simpson.

When we pulled up in front of Nicole's condo, the bus stopped. Judge Ito, in a gray suit, clambered on board and told us that we would go in groups of four or five. We were told not to pay attention to any pictures or trophies and not to talk to anyone, including each other. Note taking was OK. We would spend a few minutes in different areas of Nicole's condo. When we were finished, we would let the deputy know with raised hands. That signal would take us to the next scene.

The rules were the same, we were told, for the stop on Rockingham.

With those rules, the process was going to take some time. There were four or five groups, and each group would have about a half-hour to view the crime scene and the condo.

I peered out the buses windows at the condo. It was a nice place. The entry beyond the gate, near the street, literally overflowed with greenery. The trees and shrubs were so dense that I finally understood why no one might have heard the killings. Any cry for help, any wail of pain, would have been muffled by the tangle of growth. In that sense, it was the ideal site for a murder . . . or two.

The forecast had been for rain, but the sun was bright in the sky. It was getting warm, too warm for my sportcoat. The air conditioner on the bus didn't seem to be working. Or maybe I was warm just thinking about where we were, and what had happened there precisely eight months before. I don't know.

The signal was given for my group. We assembled on the sidewalk, the next to last group to go, waiting for the overseers to lead us through. In the distance, restrained by police, was the media horde, a couple hundred strong. I was impressed that the press corps was being kept back, away from us.

The sun beat down. It really was warm.

Finally, the deputies began to walk. We followed. We walked to the corner of Bundy Drive and Dorothy Street. We viewed the entryway to the condo from across the street. We crossed the street and arrived at the walkway.

Then it was up the walkway to the gate. I stopped. This was where two people were discovered dead. In my mind, I could see Nicole Brown Simpson in that black dress, Ron Goldman with his shirt up. I could see the blood draining down the sidewalk. And this is where it had happened. Nicole Brown Simpson's body was found at the bottom of the steps. Ron Goldman's was over to the right. In death, she looked peaceful but he looked to have died in agony. I was flooded with grief and anger. Who could have done such a thing?

I shook my head and tried to focus on the here and now. The blood was long gone, of course, but I made a point of not stepping where the victims were found. As a small child, I'd been taught not to walk where people had died, like in a graveyard where you don't walk on the graves. I stepped carefully as I looked around at the foliage. Though the sun was shining, I had no trouble imagining the gate and entryway at night, when it would be dark and no one on the street would see a thing. The area inside the gate where the killings took place seemed about eight feet by eight feet; Ron Goldman must have died like a caged animal.

After we examined the stairway and the planter area, the deputies led us down the walkway to the alley. We walked up and then back down the alley. Then they led us back to the walkway, up the stairs, and into the main entrance.

Nicole's condo was barren. There was no indication that she had lived there, no sign that two children had laughed happily inside. We saw the living room, the kitchen, the master bedroom, Sydney's bedroom, Justin's bedroom, the stairway to the garage, and the bannister, as well as the location of the ice cream cup.

From there we went into the garage. We saw it with the door open and then closed.

Leaving the garage, we were shown how it was situated in relation to the alley and walkway. Then we walked back through the condo into the garage and to the bus.

As we left, I could not shake the feeling that two people had been murdered, brutally butchered, in that small space by the gate. Someone had snuffed out their lives. It had taken virtually no time, no time at all. I could not believe that a human being could have done what had been done to two fellow beings.

On the bus, someone started to say something to me. That was against the rules, so I motioned, Stop. The thing was, I couldn't have responded anyway. My throat felt swollen shut. My eyes were watering.

I felt ashamed of myself that I had been so touched by what I'd seen. I lifted my head and looked around the bus. Everyone, it seemed, had been affected in a similar way. Heads were down. There was no sound.

We motored over to O.J.'s estate on Rockingham. We parked but didn't get off. Peering out the window, I saw O.J. at his own house, and the thought struck me that it must have been bizarre for him to be back at his own house for the first time since he'd been arrested after that chase, and knowing that, if convicted, he might never see that mansion again. It occurred to me that I hadn't seen O.J. at the crime scene. But he was here.

Soon the lawyers and the judge were standing together outside, talking. When the discussion broke up, Judge Ito boarded the bus and reminded us not to look at any of the photos inside the house.

It was hard not to notice the pictures and the trophies. They were everywhere. You would have had to be blind not to see them. I saw them, but I paid them no mind. They had no bearing on the case. We saw the entire house, from the master bedroom to the laundry room. We walked out back to Kato Kaelin's guesthouse. I had to kneel to make it underneath an air conditioner, the site where the bloody glove had been dropped. There I saw a place where it looked as if people had been jumping back and forth across the fence.

We toured the entire estate. In the courtroom the perimeter wall looked much higher than it actually stood. It didn't seem that difficult to climb over. I made a point of looking at the upstairs window to find out if I could see into O.J.'s bedroom. I took note of the doorbell buzzer, the location of the pool. I took copious amounts of notes, so detailed that to this day, I swear I could go back blindfolded and find my way around.

Back on the bus, we were given box lunches. Out the window, I saw Robert Shapiro get a plate of food from someone across the street. He seemed at ease, familiar in the neighborhood, chatting with whoever it was who gave him something to eat.

Behind the tinted windows, we ate in stark silence. Everyone, it seemed, was comparing what they'd heard in the courtroom to what they'd seen that day. Events that had been discussed and described in court now took on new life. What had happened was real. The places were real. The crime was real. At the bottom of the stairs they found Nicole Brown Simpson; just a few feet away inside the gated entryway lay Ron Goldman.

On the way back to the hotel we sat in silence. No one made a sound. No one.

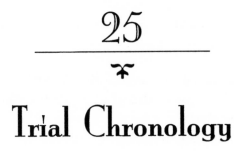

25

Trial Chronology

February 13–March 1

Monday
February 13, 1995
34th day of sequestration
Court not in session—Lincoln's birthday

Tuesday
February 14, 1995
35th day of sequestration
Jury present

MISTRIAL OF THE CENTURY

• Officer Robert Riske returned to the stand. Direct examination was conducted by Marcia Clark for the prosecution. Johnnie Cochran represented the defense team on cross-examination.

• L.A.P.D. Sergeant David Rossi, with twenty-five years on the job, was the next witness. Marcia Clark handled the questions for the prosecution. F. Lee Bailey, in his first appearance before the jury, cross-examined for the defense.

Outside of court

• Questions of juror misconduct persist and an investigation is ongoing.

• Trial expenses were noted by the Board of Supervisors, which requested that the state assist in paying for the case.

• Chief of Police Willie L. Williams, speaking before the Police Commission, said that $84,000 in overtime was accrued by police for the Sunday field trip of the Simpson jury.

Wednesday
February 15, 1995
36th day of sequestration
Jury present

• F. Lee Bailey continued his cross-examination of Sergeant Rossi, returning from yesterday.

- Ronald Phillips, an L.A.P.D. homicide detective, took the stand to testify about his part in the investigation of the crime scene. He also testified about going to the Rockingham address. He was questioned by Marcia Clark for the prosecution.

Jury not present

- In a discovery hearing outside the presence of the jury, prosecutor Rockne Harmon, a DNA legal expert, disclosed that DNA testing has matched O.J. Simpson's blood to spots found on the gate at the scene of the murders.

- The defense is charging that police planted O.J. Simpson's blood in various locations. Rockne Harmon said that Simpson's known blood sample contains preservative and that there is a test to determine the presence of the preservative. Harmon said that tests will show the absence of preservative in the blood spots.

- The judge ruled that the prosecution may keep the blood samples from the gate to test for preservative. They may also retain other samples, including the blood spots from the socks, for further testing.

Outside the court

- A.C. Cowlings, longtime best friend of O.J. Simpson, has established a 900 call-in line, which costs callers $2.99 a minute. The messages are tape recorded and do not include information about the Bronco trip in which Cowlings was the driver. He is expected to garner $1 per minute from each call.

Thursday
February 16, 1995
37th day of sequestration
Jury present

• Detective Ron Phillips resumed the stand. Cross-examination was conducted by Johnnie Cochran for the defense. Phillips was the day's only witness.

Outside the trial

• Attorney Carl Jones, representing prospective defense witness Rosa Lopez, has announced that her whereabouts are unknown at this time.

Friday
February 17, 1995
38th day of sequestration
Jury present

• Ronald Phillips remained on the stand, undergoing cross-examination from Johnnie Cochran.

• Tom Lange, L.A.P.D. detective and lead investigator in the O.J. Simpson double-homicide case, was called to the stand late in the day. Under questioning by Marcia Clark, Detective Lange identified the bloodstained glove from the scene of the crime.

• In an unusual occurrence, Judge Ito called a juror to a sidebar conference with the lawyers from both sides. Out of earshot of the other jurors and spectators, she talked to the gathering before returning to the jury box.

Outside the court

• The allegedly missing defense witness, Rosa Lopez, has been located, according to the O.J. Simpson defense team. She was seen at her daughter's place in Los Angeles and may be available to testify, according to Robert Shapiro.

Saturday
February 18, 1995
39th day of sequestration

Sunday
February 19, 1995
40th day of sequestration

Monday
February 20, 1995
41st day of sequestration
Court closed for holiday—Presidents' Day

Tuesday
February 21, 1995
42nd day of sequestration
Jury present

• Detective Tom Lange continued on the stand all day. He was the only witness. His testimony was not completed, so he will return tomorrow.

Jury not present

• Judge Lance Ito ordered Carl Jones, attorney for defense witness Rosa Lopez, to have her present in court on Friday.

Wednesday
February 22, 1995
43rd day of sequestration
Jury present

• Detective Tom Lange, in his third day on the witness stand, continued to testify under strong cross-examination by Johnnie Cochran. He was the only witness.

Jury not present

• Prosecutors filed a motion regarding prospective defense witness Kathleen Bell, who is expected to testify that Detective Mark Fuhrman made racist remarks in her presence several years ago. Bell apparently does not want to testify if she will be subject to cross-examination. The prosecution contends that the defense should not be allowed to ask Detective Fuhrman about those alleged remarks if Bell is not going to stand behind her accusations.

Thursday
February 23, 1995
44th day of sequestration
Jury not present

• The trial was delayed this morning due to the absence of prosecutor Marcia Clark, who was taking care of personal business.

• Judge Ito announced that he is going to cut down the number of hours court is in session every day, starting next week.

Jury present

• Cross-examination by Johnnie Cochran continued as Detective Tom Lange was again on the stand.

• Judge Ito interrupted cross-examination to call a sidebar after the interrogation by Cochran and the replies by Lange were contentious. There were numerous objections from the prosecution, with the hostility escalating. Judge Ito hastily ordered the jury out as the sidebar conference turned into a brouhaha. Christopher Darden was gesticulating vigorously.

There was a considerable delay due to a standoff between Judge Ito and Christopher Darden, who refused to apologize for sidebar remarks prompted by Johnnie Cochran's derogatory remarks. Darden and Ito parried back and forth. Ito cited Darden for contempt, but then vacated the citation. Finally Christopher Darden apologized, and Judge Ito apologized to him.

• The jury was excused until Monday, as Rosa Lopez was scheduled to appear on Friday.

Friday
February 24, 1995
45th day of sequestration
Jury not present

• Prospective defense witness Rosa Lopez was in court, clad in a purple sweatsuit. She was testifying in an unusual interruption in the prosecution case. Her appearance out of order was the upshot of her statement that she was leaving the country to return to El Salvador permanently, that night. She is expected to testify for O.J. Simpson, saying that she saw his Bronco parked in the street outside his house at the time of the murders.

• The defense requested that Rosa Lopez be permitted to testify while being videotaped to memorialize her statements, should she flee the country.

• Under nonvideo questioning by Christopher Darden, Lopez was caught in several outright lies and inconsistencies.

• The defense was agreeable to videotaping her testimony at 6:00 P.M., after an already extended day in court. Judge Ito wanted the jury to hear her testimony live, so he ordered the jury brought to court for the 6:00 P.M. testimony.

Jury present

• Jurors were hastily brought to court in their leisure attire, only to be told by Judge Ito that it was a false alarm. He apologized for the inconvenience, and they were returned to their sequestered housing.

• Marcia Clark reminded the judge that he had agreed she would not be subject to a late session, due to the child care needs of her two small children. Judge Ito apologized, saying he had forgotten the arrangement.

• Judge Ito extracted directly from Rosa Lopez the promise that she would return Monday morning.

Saturday
February 25, 1995
46th day of sequestration

Sunday
February 26, 1995
47th day of sequestration

Monday
February 27, 1995
48th day of sequestration
Jury not present

• Defense witness Rosa Lopez's testimony was videotaped for use later during the defense case. Lopez is an alibi witness for O.J. Simpson.

• Prosecutor Marcia Clark asked Judge Ito for sanctions against the defense for again failing to provide discovery, this time regarding a document containing an interview with Rosa Lopez from July.

• Defense private investigator Bill Pavelic was sworn in and declared that an audiotape had also been made, though Carl Douglas for the defense had stated that there was no tape.

• Judge Ito said that he will not impose sanctions until the tape of Rosa Lopez's testimony became part of the defense case. There was considerable speculation that the testimony of Rosa Lopez will not be played.

Tuesday
February 28, 1995
49th day of sequestration
Jury not present

• To accommodate the prosecution, Judge Ito granted a delay until Thursday to study the Rosa Lopez taped interview from July. The tape was turned over by private investigator Bill Pavelic.

• Part of the session was held in chambers, where the lawyers and Judge Ito played the Rosa Lopez tape. Defense witness Rosa Lopez waited to learn whether or not her video testimony would resume.

• Judge Ito ordered the defense to pay for Rosa Lopez's hotel accommodations while she is waiting to resume testimony.

• This afternoon Rosa Lopez told Judge Ito that she was tired and didn't want any more questions. He ordered her to return to court on Thursday.

Wednesday
March 1, 1995
50th day of sequestration
Jury present

• A fourth juror, Michael Knox, forty-six, an African-American courier from Long Beach, was removed from the jury by Judge Lance Ito. The reason cited was "good cause." He was replaced by a white woman, age thirty-eight, a telephone company employee.

• The judge told the reconstituted jury that their

presence would not be required for the rest of the week and that new movies would be provided for their entertainment.

• Gerald Uelmen for the defense returned to the trial after an absence of several weeks. He apologized to the court for the error in failing to turn over the required material, stating, "We screwed up."

Jury not present

• The prosecution sought further sanctions against the defense for failure to disclose evidence. Marcia Clark argued for the prosecution.

• Carl Douglas for the defense claimed that the discovery problem happened while former lead attorney Robert Shapiro was still in charge of the defense. He stated that he and Johnnie Cochran inherited the material when Cochran took over as lead attorney. The judge did not render a decision on possible sanctions.

26

Disputes and Confrontations

Tracy

February—March 1995

Rosa who?

We had no idea what was going on while Rosa Lopez held center stage. All we knew was that we were kept out of the courtroom for days on end. Once, on a Friday evening, we were summoned to the courtoom on short notice. But when we arrived, we were told it was a false alarm and taken back to the hotel.

The long layoff was a drag. It exacerbated the isolation we all felt. It underscored the sense of how unreal the whole thing was—being stuck in the same rooms, going to the same places, seeing only the same faces, day after day after day. Disputes, most of them unbelievably petty, erupted with regularity. Cliques formed fast, and feelings were always being hurt. Suspicion frequently gave way to outright hostility.

Living in such close quarters, with so many different personalities, conflict proved inevitable.

Consider: One juror had unbelievably bad breath. This sounds truly petty, I know. But his breath was so bad it was indescribable. What if you had to share space with someone and had to hold your nose or retch every time you got close? Now imagine being around this stench every day of every week. Or sharing meals. Not so funny anymore, right? The easiest thing to do was to limit one's contact with the guy. No one really wanted to ostracize him; he was a decent guy. But it couldn't be helped.

Several jurors made a point of ignoring one of the other jurors from the beginning, after she announced in the elevator, "Hey, guys . . . I'm gay," as we were riding up to the food room. I still don't know why she chose that moment to announce her sexual orientation, or why she felt it important to let us in on the fact in such a dramatic fashion. But she did. No one said a word. Well, really, what was there to say? Conversation stopped for a heartbeat, and then it picked right up. From that moment on, that juror was treated with a cool reserve by several others. I couldn't have cared less, and I enjoyed her company. But it was obvious that others had difficulty embracing her lifestyle. There were winks, nods, and jokes about conjugal visits.

Another juror had a habit that was truly, truly annoying. She would twirl her hair. She would twirl it even when she was going through the food line at the hotel, and strands of hair would fall into the food. People complained. After a while she got the hint and took to going through the line last. That really didn't solve the problem, though, because a lot of people went back for seconds. When they got there, they would find hairs in the serving dishes.

People tried to tolerate things they wouldn't even think of tolerating with their spouses. For a while, good manners helped considerably, especially at the beginning. I swear, I never spent as much time apologizing as I did around these people.

"Oops, I stepped on your toes. Sorry."

"Oh, sorry, my elbow got you there."

"Excuse me, I accidentally dropped that. I'm sorry."

Trust me, I wasn't the only one apologizing. We all were. Tracy Hampton, who sat in Seat 2 immediately next to me, used to step on my heels a lot.

"I'm sorry, excuse me," she'd say.

"Don't worry about it," I'd reply.

The lady in back of me in the jury box, Number 98, would occasionally kick the back of my chair.

"I'm sorry," she'd say.

"No problem."

After a while, though, everyone's patience wore thin. An apology or an "excuse me" was not enough.

At the front end of the food line at the hotel was a

small container of toothpicks. I would always get one after eating, go back to the table, and use the toothpick. This drove Farron Chavarria crazy. But I didn't know it until the one night when she jumped all over me.

"Don't pick your teeth at the table!" she blurted out. "You remind me of my dad when you do that. Yuck. Would you please go do that somewhere else?"

"Oh, I'm sorry," I said. "It won't happen again."

I put the toothpick in my pocket. I jumped up to go outside to the patio, but the door was locked. There was nowhere for me to go. I felt stuck and trapped. She just glared at me.

Earlier in the meal, I actually had to hunt down the container of toothpicks. Instead of being on the buffet line, they were sitting on one of the dining tables. Number 165, the seventy-two-year-old African-American man, had moved them there.

"May I have a toothpick, please?" I asked when I saw the container there.

"Leave those alone," he ordered.

"I think," I said, "that these are for everybody."

"Not for you," he said.

I picked up the container, took one, and put them back where they were supposed to be.

"Thank you very much," I said. He glared.

The next day, in the food room at the courthouse, I found a big box of toothpicks left by the lunch caterers. I got a big handful and put the picks in my pocket to take back to the hotel. That evening, I saw Number 165 and, intending to mend fences, winked conspiratorially and told him I'd gotten something for all of us. He didn't hear me correctly, never looked down at the toothpicks, and only saw me winking at him as if I was making fun of him, adding insult to injury. He was furious and ended up mumbling about me for a while in the back of the courthouse elevator.

Grudges erupted, over the smallest things and assumed an importance that was way out of proportion to their real significance.

On the patio one evening after dinner, Catherine Murdoch and Francine Florio-Bunten were out for a walk, more like a speed-walk for exercise. Jeanette Harris and Number 1233 were also out for a walk, but they were just ambling about. I was out there for a run. The patio was crowded. Zipping through the crowds, Catherine opted to try to speed between Jeanette and Number 1233 instead of going around them. I had done the same thing myself any number of times; so had Catherine. Whenever she or I would find ourselves behind them, we would say, "Excuse me," and rush our way through. Sometimes they would move. Sometimes they wouldn't, and you'd have to go around or wait until you got to a wider place on the patio where you could go around. This night, for whatever reason, it really irked Jeanette when Catherine maneuvered through. Jeanette claimed she was shoved. And then the next thing we knew, there was talk that it was a racial incident— Catherine is white, while Jeanette and Number 1233 are African-American.

That wasn't the way I saw it. It didn't appear to have anything at all to do with the color of anyone's skin. It was like the toothpick affair between me and

Number 165. I'm white, he's black. But we were living under so much pressure, and the atmosphere was so poisoned by paranoia and suspicion, that it was tempting to ascribe a sinister meaning to things that had absolutely nothing to do with race.

There were other incidents along those lines—things that had nothing to do with race and everything to do with personality conflicts that turned into more than what they were and caused hurt feelings all around.

Number 247 had words with Willie. I also saw Number 247 have words with Michael Knox. I really don't know what either of the arguments was about, but it seems hard to believe that they were driven by race. All three are African-American.

Then there was the time that Number 1290, the sixty-year-old white woman, sat down at a dinner table and three of the black jurors who had been there cleared right out. Racial animosity? No. Misunderstanding? Yes. When Number 1290 was in line, one of the jurors at that table had said, "Why don't you come and sit with us?"

"Fine," she said, "I'll do that."

She fixed her plate and went to sit down. Just as she was doing so, the three black jurors got up.

"Well, I guess, you know, if you ever want to empty out a table, just call me over," Number 1290 had said.

The three black jurors, it turned out, had finished eating and had decided at that moment that it was time to go out onto the patio for a walk.

"Well, you know, they have a problem. It's not you," someone told 1290.

But her feelings clearly were hurt. Later, it turned out, she even complained to Judge Ito about it.

Though these and other incidents weren't racially motivated, it would be naive to say that the jury dynamics weren't affected by race. For instance, the jury quickly fractured into three main cliques, divided along racial lines. Considerable friction developed among the cliques. I still believe, however, that it wasn't about race but instead was the product of a clash between strong personalities in each of the groups.

In Clique 1: Farron Chavarria, Francine Florio-Bunten, Number 19, and Number 1290.

In Clique 2: Willie Cravin, Jeanette Harris, Number 1233, and, to a lesser extent, Number 984, and Number 2179.

In Clique 3: Number 230, Number 984, and Number 98.

The friction between Willie and Farron was considerable. It got to the point where she complained to the judge that he bumped her in the courthouse elevators, brushed up against her in the jury room, and stared at her.

There were also sparks between Willie and Francine. She complained to the judge, too, saying that she had inadvertently tripped one day on his foot while entering the jury box and he had responded by saying that if it happened again, he would trip her.

Number 1290 got into the act as well. She complained to Judge Ito that Willie was staring at her, too.

There was friction between cliques 1 and 2 virtually

every day, and almost always it was over the same things: movies and exercise.

As the incident with Catherine and Jeanette highlighted, the patio was often an unsuitable site for serious running. The other options, quite obviously, were to exercise at a different time or at a different place. I usually opted for a jog at five in the morning, if I could convince one of the overseers to hop out of bed.

The other jurors were far more interested in the workout room elsewhere in the hotel, the one available to hotel guests. Since hotel management deemed it off-limits before six in the morning, the only time the jury had access to it was after ten at night. Frequently, Clique 1, joined sometimes by Number 63, the young white woman in Seat 11, would troop down there at that time and monopolize the equipment—the treadmill, stairstepper, rowing machine, bicycle, and barbells. They would stay there until eleven, when it was time to be back in our rooms, giving no one else the opportunity to use the machines.

At some point, Judge Ito convinced someone to donate some exercise equipment, and the overseers set up a workout room on the fifth floor of the hotel. It had less equipment—a stairstepper, bike and treadmill—but the overseers announced that all workouts were to be done in there from then on. Clique 1 didn't miss a beat. The group quickly took over that new room at nine each night.

While they were sweating, they'd talk about the others on the jury. They sniped, mostly, while they plotted how to dictate to the entire jury what movies we'd see.

When we were first sequestered, the only movies we could see were those available through the hotel TV system. We could watch them on only one television set, which had been set up in a room down the fifth-floor hall.

As any business traveler can tell you, if you stay at one hotel long enough, you go through all the movies on the hotel system pretty quickly. That's what happened to us, especially in the beginning when we were not frequently in court. When January turned to February, the hotel rotated the movie titles on the system, which was cause for excitement. It lasted, however, for only a few days because there weren't many new movies. We begged for a VCR.

A few weeks later, after someone wrote a letter to Judge Ito the VCR appeared. It was set up in that same room down the hall. Videos from Blockbuster also began to appear.

Videos also came flowing in from the jurors' families. The overseers exercised their authority and screened each video. For instance, Number 19 was given a copy of one of the NFL playoff games. Unfortunately, his pals had spiced it up by cutting X-rated shots into the football action between the plays.

So much for regular access to videos from anywhere but Blockbuster.

At any rate, a few weeks later we asked for a second VCR. There was simply too much conflict over which movie would air each night. We'd decided to take a vote, majority rules, and what that spawned was a system that reinforced the power of the cliques.

Clique 1 had four votes. Clique 2 had five. Clique 2 would win. Simple as that.

The four in Clique 1 were forever asking me to vote their way. If they could get me and Number 63, who was working out with them, they would win the movie vote, six to five.

I declined. I did not want to be a part of their group or any group. That's exactly what I told them. I had made up my mind from the very start that I didn't want to be a part of anyone's group. I've always been a loner, not a group person. And I figured that if we were sequestered for months and months, someone would have to mediate. I'd always been a good mediator.

They didn't buy it.

What made the problem worse was that some of the members of Clique 2 would vote for a particular movie, then decide they had better things to do than watch it. They'd leave the room, consistently leaving Willie and perhaps one or two others to watch the movie. Willie liked to watch movies in absolute silence, and when people would talk while the movie was going on, he would order them to be silent. Willie was not shy about expressing his strong preference for quiet in the movie room. I also like watching movies in a quiet room, and I frankly liked watching them with Willie.

At any rate, Willie and his agenda did not sit well with those in Clique 1. After a letter to Judge Ito, a second VCR did appear. It was set up with another

TV in the first room by the Control Point in the hallway. Then came the Clique 1 power play. Clique 1 adopted the new room and it somehow came to be that all newly arrived Blockbuster videos were shown first in that room. Only after they aired there would they move back to the original movie room.

This did not sit well with Willie, Jeanette, or the others in their group. Or me, for that matter.

One day, Number 19 was complaining to me about his troubles with Willie, and I said, "Wait a minute. I get along with Willie. Let me talk to him."

"No, I'll handle it," Number 19 said.

"Well, hey, I like Willie," I said.

Number 19 looked at me. From that moment on, I was on the outs with him.

Mind you, I was still sitting at the dinner table with Number 19, Number 1290, Francine, and Farron. Beats me why. Number 1290 once said to me, "Why don't you move to another table?" I answered, "I don't want to."

She and I ultimately came to disagree about anything and everything. She rarely missed an opportunity to let me know that we had virtually nothing in common. If I said at dinner that such-and-such a movie was good, she'd say, "Oh, it's not so great." One time, she asked me about my taste in music. I said I liked John Denver. "I don't like him," she said. Another time we were talking and I put forth my opinion that we were all God's children, all one big family here on the planet. "I don't go along with that," she said. If I said, "Excuse me," she would say, "You're always apologizing."

As for Farron, it seemed that everything I did irritated her, too. At dinner, I used to put my feet up on the rung of the chair next to mine, the same way I would put my feet up after lunch in the food room. I have bad circulation and it eased the pressure on my feet to elevate them. That irritated her. I put pepper on my food. That irritated her. The way I chewed my food irritated her. I would swish water around my mouth after eating because I just can't stand food particles in my teeth. That irritated her. It irritated her that I did not talk much and I kept to myself. I think it got to the point that the way I breathed irritated her.

One day in the food room, I was lying on one of the couches, reading a newspaper. Nearby was a table at which Farron, Francine, and Number 19 were sitting. The paper was situated in front of me in such a way that I was reading the upper right-hand corner; in the background was Farron's face.

"What are you looking at?" she said.

I changed my focus to look at her, and said, "The paper. I'm reading the paper."

"I've been watching you," she said, "and I've been wondering why you're staring at me. I looked at you a couple times and you were staring."

I thought to myself, how can anyone tell if they're being stared at unless they're staring themselves at the person who's supposed to be staring? I sighed and went back to the newspaper. It was the culture of paranoia. We were all so edgy.

With Number 19, all pretense at civility nearly vanished. One night I came down to dinner and I said hello to everyone at the table. In response, he said to Number 1386, the young female alternate juror, "Well, I guess I lose my bet with you." Apparently, they'd had a bet about whether I would say one word. I had been quiet for several straight meals, and that had prompted the wager.

"You guys really ought to make sure I'm not here when you make a bet about me," I said. Tears appeared in Number 1386's eyes. Everyone was so on edge that every little thing turned big.

I turned to her and said, "I'm sorry. I didn't mean to hurt you, but there are people in here who are truly vicious."

"Are you," Number 19 said, "talking about me?"

"No. I'm not. I'm really not." I really wasn't. I was thinking about Number 1290. Until that instant, it had not occurred to me that Number 19 might have made the bet at my expense.

"Well, we're going to have to talk about this later. Just you and me privately," he said.

"No, I don't think so. I don't trust you."

Number 19 had told everyone on any number of occasions that he was a black belt in some form of the martial arts, and he had all these karate or judo T-shirts, whatever they were. Who wanted to meet in private with someone who had hands of stone?

After considering what I'd said to him, Number 19 abruptly jumped up from the table. "Get the f— away from me!" he said.

I couldn't believe this was happening. I didn't think I could have provoked anyone this severely. He sat back down and said, "Just stay the f— away from me."

"That's going to be hard to do," I replied.

He said something else, I don't remember what, and by then all the overseers were watching.

"Are you threatening me?" I asked him.

Two of the overseers came over and escorted him out of the dining room. I walked over to the buffet line and got more food.

In court, Number 19 and I still had to sit next to each other. At the hotel, we stubbornly sat at the same dinner table. I apologized and offered to shake hands, but he refused. There were no more words between us.

✢

With so much tension in the air, I decided we ought to have a session to talk everything out. No one appointed me boss, I know, but it simply seemed like the sensible thing to do.

It's just my nature. I try to help people. It doesn't always turn out right, but I try.

Earlier in the trial, I tried to help when I noticed what was happening with one of the jurors. Whenever we'd eat lunch, this juror was always watching to make sure that she could go into the bathroom by herself. When she came back out, her eyes would be watery, and she was dabbing at her mouth or reapplying her lipstick. And she had a distinct smell about her as if she'd been throwing up. She would walk right by me and I would smell it.

One day, instead of taking a nap after lunch, I happened to be standing by the water fountain on the wall, just outside the women's restroom. I could hear her in there. Apparently, one of the others heard her, too, because she ran in there to help.

Shortly thereafter, I approached another of the female jurors, one of her friends, and said, "I have a problem. I like to help people when I can. Let me tell you about what I've seen and heard. I don't know if it's appropriate for me to say anything to her."

"It's none of your business," the friend said after I finished my story. "I'm not going to say anything to her. You certainly shouldn't."

After that, though, I felt I had to report what I'd seen and heard to Judge Ito. I knew from my wife's experiences while working at Jenny Craig that we conceivably could be talking about a life-threatening condition, and I could not live with my conscience if someone needed help and I didn't do my best to get her help. I sent the judge a note. He called me into his chambers, we talked about it, and he said, "OK, we'll look into it."

That was the last I heard of it.

Given the unresolved outcome of that effort, perhaps I ought to have given more thought to the notion of a group session at which we could each air out our feelings and complaints. Instead, I plowed ahead. The way I saw it, there was no downside to a session at which we could get the bickering and the personality conflicts out in the open, acknowledge them, and move on.

One day in the jury room, as soon as the door

closed, fingers started pointing at Number 1290. She had written a letter to Judge Ito asking that the deputies who served as our overseers on the weekends wear civilian clothes rather than uniforms, to eliminate one aspect of the prisonlike surroundings. Almost everyone had discussed this idea in private and agreed it had merit. Number 1290 decided to do something about it. She wrote Judge Ito a letter and he ultimately granted the request. The problem was, Number 1290 hadn't told anyone what she was doing. As soon as word got around, all hell broke loose. When the door closed that day on the jury room, the accusations came fast and furious.

"What was that letter about?"

"Why did you request something without first consulting the rest of us?"

"Don't ever do that again!"

When things quieted down, and people returned to their card games or their books, I said, "Excuse me, may I have everyone's attention." Everyone looked at me.

"First of all, I want to make it perfectly clear that I do not want the foreman's job. That is not what I'm doing. But I know, and everybody in here knows, that we have some personality conflicts and some tension. We need to talk about it. We are a big family here and we're going to have to get along. You can pick your friends but you can't pick your family, and that's what we are."

Everyone agreed, except for Number 1290 (who cornered me later to tell me we weren't all family). I suggested that someone say something about me, just to get the ball rolling. Number 230 mentioned that she'd been upset at me in January because I had been able to bring my computer to the hotel when she hadn't been able to bring hers. She considered that a double standard and resented me. "I've got my computer now," she said, explaining that she also had been asked to sign an affidavit. I told her that I'd felt badly for a while because I felt she had blamed me for a double standard.

"I didn't know you felt bad about a little thing like that," Number 230 said in front of the group.

"You see," I said. "It's a little thing, but this is why we need to talk about things like this. If we don't, they're going to get completely out of hand."

From there, we talked about the situation with the movies. Nothing got resolved, although we did receive a second VCR.

A week later, I tried again. "Excuse me, ladies and gentlemen," I said in the jury room. "I think we ought to have another meeting."

Number 1233 said it bothered people that I would put my feet up on the tables in the phone room. "You're right, and I apologize," I said. "I forget that I'm not at home. I put them up because I have bad circulation in my lower legs. Putting them up makes them feel better, keeps my feet from going numb. But I do apologize."

"All right," Number 1233 said. "I understand. But the rest of us don't like it when you do that."

"OK, fine, that's a good starting point," I said. "What else?"

The movies came up again and someone mentioned the machines in the workout room. The meeting turned into a bunch of jabbering. Nothing was resolved.

So, the following week, I tried again.

"Excuse me, ladies and gentlemen," I said. "We haven't had a session for a while. Why don't we talk about some problems?"

Voices became loud. Pointing at Farron, Willie said, "You guys make noise and bump my chair when we're trying to watch the movie."

She got upset and delivered a lesson in manners: "You don't point at people. You point at things."

Things got louder. Francine jumped up and ran out the door and hollered for an overseer. "We need a deputy in here right now," she yelled out into the hall.

An overseer came in and said, "What's going on here? You guys aren't supposed to be talking about anything."

"Listen," I said, "we're just airing some problems."

"Did you instigate this thing?" he said to me.

"Not really, it was a mutual thing," I said.

"You're not the foreman," the overseer said. "You're not supposed to have a foreman yet."

"I know that," I said with a sigh. "We haven't picked a foreman yet. I don't want the job anyhow. We were just talking."

No, we weren't, actually. There were no more meetings.

From then on it grew to resemble the famous book *Lord of the Flies*.

❡

The deputies were not all bad. I honestly did like Jex, the head deputy. He was reasonable and I could talk to him. I felt the same about Sergeant Smith. Another of the overseers, Deputy G-12, as we called him, was an OK guy, too. Antranik Geuvjehizian was his real name. He was shot and killed in July as he tried to investigate a break-in at his neighbor's house. I mourned his death.

Too often, however, the overseers were arbitrary or rigid. Some specialized in treating us as if we were a huge inconvenience in their lives.

I never could understand that, especially considering the overtime they must have been drawing while keeping watch over us.

In general, if we wanted something, the response was "No," or "Write a letter to the judge."

For instance, every one of the juror rooms at the hotel had a refrigerator. Each of the refrigerators was locked. I asked if I could use my refrigerator. "No. You're not allowed to do that." I wasn't interested in popping a few brews each night because I couldn't get them anyhow. I merely wanted to keep sodas or water in the room. So I picked the lock and used the refrigerator.

Down the hall, in the original movie room, was a big refrigerator, constantly stocked with soft drinks. The deputies were asked for a great big jug of bottled water. Surprisingly, it was provided. But the movie room was kept under lock and key, so the water was off-limits unless the door was open. This was senseless. If you were thirsty and wanted good, clean water, you were forbidden to get it because it was kept behind a locked door.

One evening, I pointed to the bottled water and said to one of the overseers, "Let's take this out into the hall." And I started to lug it out the door.

"What do you think you're doing?" the overseer said.

"Moving the water cooler out into the hallway so that when you lock this door we can still get water."

"No," he said. "If it gets moved, we'll move it."

"Why can't you move it now?"

"Because I said so."

I wish I could say that this was the only time that any of us were talked to like an adult would speak to a small child. It was embarrassing and humiliating to be spoken to in such a fashion. But it was not uncommon.

One weekend, we took a trip to Target, the department store. I was all excited to get out of the hotel and shop for my wife. When we got there, the overseers divided us into groups—five jurors to one deputy. They told us to stay away from the books and magazines and made arrangements for us to bring all our stuff to a particular register. Then we were off.

Each of the deputies looked very nervous. The one leading our group told us to stay within sight of one another and, most importantly, where he could see us. I was with four women. One of them needed batteries for a video game. Then we saw the card rack. There were two racks, I believe, and I love buying cards for Judy, and I lost myself in reading the cards.

It was just before Valentine's Day and I was looking for the right card. Inadvertently, I slipped around a corner and out of the overseer's sight. I couldn't have been more than fifteen feet away.

When he saw me, he proceeded to chew me out, right there in the store, right there in front of the other jurors and a crowd of other shoppers.

"I told you to stay in my sight," he barked. "What were you doing? Did you not understand my instructions? Was I not clear? What did you think you were doing?"

This really hurt my feelings. Then I got really angry at him for directing his feelings at me in a way that was meant to put me down. I didn't say anything, but the entire trip was ruined. I tagged along with the women to get hair coloring, then browsed with them through the women's fashions, things like that.

After about an hour, as we were approaching the checkout counter, the deputy said to me, "Is there anywhere you want to go?"

"No. I'm through, thanks. I don't need to get hollered at anymore."

I had completely forgotten to get my wife a birthday card for March, and didn't know when we would get to go shopping again.

About the only time the overseers didn't consider us a pain was when we asked to see the Super Bowl. They wanted to see it, too. We had popcorn and potato chips and the room was packed. Everyone had a good time. What a rarity.

In fairness, Judge Ito did try to ease the tension of being confined with a variety of distractions, including a steady procession of entertainers. Some of them were truly magnificent.

Leona Boyd, the classical guitarist, put on an amazing show. She even gave me a CD to listen to, which I treasured.

Roger Williams, the pianist, was wonderful. "Hi, I'm Rog," he said when we were introduced.

"I'm 602," I replied. Later, he told the whole group that he thought he could identify with what it was like to be sequestered. He was forever on the road, he said, living out of a suitcase in cookie-cutter hotels, practicing until all hours and never really getting out of the hotel room.

A magician, Brian Gillis, performed an amazing trick. He actually got us to admit our first names. He used us as props for his tricks and asked—I'm sure without him even thinking about it—what our names were, the way any magician would do. Intriguingly, we responded with names, not our jury numbers. None of the overseers did anything about it.

Of course, there were always movies to see. Even with the constant bickering and politicking, we did manage to see a bunch of first-rate films: *The Shawshank Redemption, I Love Trouble, Blown Away, True Lies, The Specialist, It Could Happen to You, Tombstone, The Flintstones, Grumpy Old Men, The Lion King, Maverick, Rudy, Quiz Show,* and *Philadelphia.*

When we watched *Philadelphia*, there was no trouble maintaining quiet in the room. It was a serious movie, and the mood in the room was somber. When the movie ended, everyone cheered out loud against the Establishment.

✶

The movies and the entertainers were distractions from the tensions, stress, isolation, and paranoia. I felt it constantly and intensely. And I wasn't just imagining things. Some days in the courtroom, I felt a powerful sense that I was being watched. Of course, most eyes in the audience were frequently turned toward the jury box, looking for any sort of telling twitch, but it was more than that. I couldn't put my finger on it.

It wasn't until months after I was dismissed that I learned Judge Ito had been focusing a surveillance camera on me. While I had, and have, the utmost respect for the judge, I find it hard to comprehend why a private citizen called to duty would find himself the object of a judge's secret TV camera. What could he pick up on TV that he couldn't see by looking at me a few feet away in the courtroom? A *Los Angeles Times* headline hit it right on the mark: "Jurors are 'Defendants' in the Private Trial You Never See."

The judge was forever holding meetings in his chambers as well. Some of them were obviously about the jury, because various jurors would troop to and from the jury room to chambers. But some of them were just as obviously secret investigations about the jurors because they resulted in the dismissal of members of the jury. Nothing fueled the paranoia like the dismissal of a juror.

I'd see a juror called out of the jury room. He or she wouldn't return. We'd file into the courtroom and the seat would be so noticeably empty. I'd think, wow, what did they do? I wondered if they had maps that they couldn't explain or something else. Was it something innocent? Maybe Judge Ito simply didn't buy their explanation.

One of the first two jurors dismissed was Number 320, who used to sit next to me at the dinner table. I loved chitchatting with her. The other of the first two was the guy from Hertz, Number 228. I liked talking to him, too. Third to go was Catherine Murdoch. We sat together at dinner, too. It seemed that the people I sat next to, the people I associated with, were being plucked out and sent home. I thought, was it me? Maybe I was the problem. Perhaps the word on the jury was not to get friendly with me. If you did, you'd get bounced.

On March 1, Michael Knox was excused. He and I had been friendly, I thought.

I couldn't help but wonder when he disappeared that we had not seen the last dismissal. And I wondered: Who would be next?

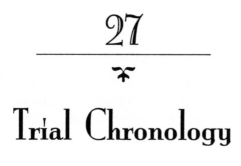

27

Trial Chronology

March 2–March 17

Thursday
March 2, 1995
51st day of sequestration
Jury not present

• Defense witness Rosa Lopez, testifying out of order while being videotaped, contradicted herself repeatedly under cross-examination by prosecutor Christopher Darden. She denied having made certain statements in a TV interview, but the interview was played back for her, clearly indicating that she had made those remarks.

• Rosa Lopez was caught in numerous discrepancies pertaining to her behavior, her credentials, and her testimony regarding the night of June 12, 1994. She admitted to telling lies on the stand when she said she had not filed for unemployment.

• Although Rosa Lopez said she required an interpreter, she frequently answered questions without waiting for the translation, and she spoke to the police and TV interviewers in English. She has been in the United States twenty-five years.

• Lead defense attorney Johnnie Cochran was accused of sending hand signals to Rosa Lopez. He was forced to attempt to explain these gestures to Judge Ito. The signals were televised nationally by the courtroom video camera to home viewers. Cochran alleged he was signaling the court reporter. Judge Ito, who had seen the hand gestures, attempted to verbalize what the signals resembled for the court reporter, causing laughter in the courtroom.

• Rosa Lopez said repeatedly that she could not remember telling a friend that she, too, could get $5,000 for saying she saw the Bronco on the night of June 12.

• Rosa Lopez said in Spanish, "I don't remember, sir", in answer to questions more than fifty times.

She vacillated on the time she alleged she saw O.J. Simpson's Bronco parked on the street.

• Cross-examination of Rosa Lopez will continue tomorrow.

Outside of court

• Controversy continued over the custody battle between lead prosecutor Marcia Clark and her former husband, Gordon Clark, over their two children. Los Angeles District Attorney Gil Garcetti appealed to members of the media to grant her privacy regarding her personal life.

Friday
March 3, 1995
52nd day of sequestration
Jury not present

• Rosa Lopez concluded her testimony and prepared to depart for her native El Salvador. In a defense attempt to rehabilitate their witness, who admitted to numerous lies and uttered more than ninety replies of "I don't remember," Johnnie Cochran asked what she meant by "I don't remember." She stated, "When I am saying 'I don't remember' I am saying 'no.' " She attributed this to different dialects being spoken in Latin America.

• Judge Lance Ito fined and sanctioned the defense

team. Both lead attorney Johnnie Cochran and his associate Carl Douglas were fined $950 each for their failure to provide the prosecution with prompt disclosure regarding the defense witness Rosa Lopez. Judge Ito cited Johnnie Cochran for making "untrue representations to the court and reckless disregard for the truth."

• Judge Ito said that if the defense elects to use the videotaped testimony of Rosa Lopez, he will advise the jury of a further sanction. He will admonish the jury about defense misconduct as follows: "This was a violation of the law, and the cause of the delay. You may consider the effect of this delay in disclosure, if any, upon the credibility of the witness involved and give to it the weight to which you feel it is entitled."

Outside of court

• O.J. Simpson defense lawyer F. Lee Bailey, interviewed by Larry King on CNN, declared that the defense would use the Rosa Lopez videotape in the defense case.

Saturday
March 4, 1995
53rd day of sequestration

Sunday
March 5, 1995
54th day of sequestration

Monday
March 6, 1995
55th day of sequestration
Jury present

• The jury returned to court today to hear testimony after an eleven day hiatus, interrupted only by a brief court appearance for the dismissal of a juror and the seating of an alternate.

• The first witness to take the stand for the prosecution today, as the trial got back on track, was Mark Storfer, who was a neighbor of Nicole Brown Simpson. He was called out of order (before Detective Tom Lange resumed his previously interrupted testimony) because he now lives in another state. His testimony centered on barking-dog evidence. He was cross-examined by Johnnie Cochran.

• Following Mark Storfer, Detective Lange returned to the stand, under cross-examination by Johnnie Cochran.

• The afternoon session of the trial was delayed for an hour due to a bomb scare. A suspicious briefcase was found in the building, necessitating the closure of three floors and the elevator banks in the Criminal Courts Building.

• Johnnie Cochran questioned Detective Lange regarding Faye Resnick in an attempt to advance a defense theory that Nicole Simpson was killed because she was mistaken for her friend Faye Resnick, a drug user, by the murderer. Detective Lange said there was no evidence of a drug connection and "in this particular case we had another direction to go."

Outside of court

• Superior Court Judge Robert W. Parkin temporarily sealed the divorce case file in Clark v. Clark. The hearing was continued for one week. The motion to seal was made by lawyers for Marcia Clark.

Tuesday
March 7, 1995
56th day of sequestration
Jury present

• Detective Tom Lange took the witness stand for his sixth day of testimony to detail his conclusion that one killer had slaughtered both Nicole Brown Simpson and Ron Goldman. He observed that the same method was used to kill both of them: throat slashing and stabbing. He explained that there was only one set of bloody shoeprints leading from the crime scene. Lange disputed the defense theory that the crime was drug-related. He articulated the reasons that this crime scene evidence did not match the factors usually present at drug-related killings.

• Detective Lange testified that the evidence indicated that Ron Goldman did not strike his assailant, but was thrashing around in the confined area where he was trapped by the killer.

• A photo used to show the killer's bloody footprint included a portion of the body of victim Ron Goldman, bringing his sister, Kim, to silent tears.

Jury not present

• Rockne Harmon for the prosecution informed the court of DNA tests that indicated that the fingernail scrapings from victim Nicole Brown Simpson were her own blood. The scrapings are still undergoing further tests.

• Barry Scheck, DNA legal expert for the defense, complained that the prosecution had withheld results from them. Marcia Clark pointed out to Judge Ito that the defense had their own expert monitoring all the tests, so if they were unaware of results due to lack of communication with their own people, it was not the fault of the prosecution.

• Judge Ito opined that the prosecution had not acted in bad faith, but he permitted Barry Scheck to draft an instruction, to be read to the jury at a later time, to disregard that part of the testimony containing reference to the fingernail scrapings.

• Robert Tourtelot, attorney for Detective Mark Fuhrman, made a brief appearance to argue against a defense request for access to Fuhrman's police Internal Affairs records. The judge read the Fuhrman records in chambers but did not issue a ruling. Fuhrman is expected to take the stand tomorrow.

Outside of court

• Defense witness Rosa Lopez returned to her native country, El Salvador. She was hounded by the press and frequently addressed them in English. She issued forth insults in both Spanish and English before departing for a remote farm.

Wednesday
March 8, 1995
57th day of sequestration
Jury present

• Detective Tom Lange spent the entire day on the witness stand, his seventh, undergoing additional cross-examination by Johnnie Cochran. Then it was Marcia Clark's turn again. Her questioning was interrupted repeatedly by objections from Johnnie Cochran.

• Detective Lange replied to Johnnie Cochran's question regarding a "Colombian necklace," that he had heard of it. The correct term is *Colombian necktie*.

Jury not present

• Judge Ito will allow the defense to peruse two

L.A.P.D. files compiled by the Internal Affairs department on Detective Mark Fuhrman, expected to begin
testifying tomorrow. Both sides are prohibited from
revealing the contents of the police files.

• In a sidebar conference, Johnnie Cochran
broached the subject of further juror misconduct.

Thursday
March 9, 1995
58th day of sequestration
Jury present

• Detective Tom Lange ended his eighth day on the
witness stand, concluding his lengthy testimony as
stoicly as he had spoken throughout.

• Patti Goldman, stepmother of Ron Goldman, testified that a marketing list, found in a paper bag used
to collect the victim's work clothing from his apartment, was hers.

• Detective Mark Fuhrman was sworn in and
began his testimony under questioning by Marcia
Clark. He denied knowing a woman named Kathleen
Bell, who claims he made racist remarks in her presence many years ago.

Jury not present

• Judge Lance Ito cautioned the attorneys not to

make speaking objections or they would be subject to fines.

Outside of court

• F. Lee Bailey, who will be conducting the cross-examination of Detective Fuhrman, said that the defense will call a witness who will testify that Detective Fuhrman was acquainted with Kathleen Bell. Bailey said, in response to a reporter's question, that hopefully his cross-examination would amount to an assassination of Detective Fuhrman's character.

• Detective Fuhrman was escorted to and from court by several uniformed officers, who accompanied him on a private elevator. Several detectives were present in court to show their support for the veteran officer.

Friday
March 10, 1995
59th day of sequestration
Jury present

• Under questioning by Marcia Clark, Detective Mark Fuhrman detailed his activities at the Bundy crime scene and the Rockingham estate in the early morning hours following the double homicide.

• Marcia Clark gave the jurors another Friday cliff-hanger when she ended her questioning of Detective

Fuhrman with a dramatic presentation, just before the jury began their weekend. She showed Detective Fuhrman items from O.J. Simpson's Bronco, including a large heavy-duty plastic bag, a used shovel, and an old towel. She also had him identify a wooden slat with a nail protruding from it, which was found on the ground near the Bronco. The jury was excused for the weekend and returned to sequestration without hearing any explanation of the items identified by the witness.

Jury not present

• The prosecution asked Judge Ito to require F. Lee Bailey to reveal the name of the individual he said he is planning to call as a witness to substantiate the expected testimony of Kathleen Bell.

Saturday
March 11, 1995
60th day of sequestration

Sunday
March 12, 1995
61st day of sequestration

Monday
March 13, 1995
62nd day of sequestration

Jury present

• Marcia Clark ended her questioning of Detective Mark Fuhrman, and F. Lee Bailey began his cross-examination for the defense. He started in a subdued manner, which was expected to elevate to the more theatrical, bombastic style he has already displayed in this trial.

Jury not present

• F. Lee Bailey told Judge Ito that the defense hopes to prove that Detective Fuhrman is a racist who planted evidence. Marcia Clark countered that the defense will never be able to offer proof to the court that Detective Fuhrman planted anything.

Jury present

• Detective Fuhrman, under questioning by F. Lee Bailey, said he does not recognize Kathleen Bell from a photo and from television as anyone he has met. Bailey revealed the name of the witness he says will corroborate the statements of Kathleen Bell. Her name is Andrea Terry. She is living in Provo, Utah, at this time. Bailey accelerated his questioning with tinges of sarcasm and sharpness of tone, but Detective Fuhrman seemed unfazed.

Outside of court

• In the Clark v. Clark divorce case, Judge Robert

Parkin released the file that has been sealed since July 1994 by order of Judge Robert Mallano. The decision was made at an in-camera hearing attended by lawyers for Marcia Clark and her former husband, Gordon Clark.

Tuesday
March 14, 1995
63rd day of sequestration
Jury present

• Detective Mark Fuhrman maintained his composure throughout stepped-up cross-examination by F. Lee Bailey. Bailey, given to lavish gesticulation and stentorian tone, was unable to rile the calm professionalism of Detective Fuhrman.

• In an overly theatrical presentation, F. Lee Bailey placed a box on the table with great pomp and produced from it an everyday school supplies–style binder, which contained nothing more than the preliminary hearing transcript of Detective Fuhrman's testimony. Announcing to Judge Ito that he was about to do so, Bailey then handed out copies to the other attorneys. Hearing and trial transcripts are a matter of public record.

Jury not present

• Judge Ito ruled that the defense may question Detective Fuhrman about racial slurs he may have

uttered and also whether he made derogatory remarks about interracial couples.

• The defense lawyers were threatened with further sanctions by Judge Ito for failing to turn over the
notes from interviews with some of their witnesses.

• F. Lee Bailey told Judge Ito that he had spoken
with scheduled defense witness Max Cordoba, "Marine to Marine," and that he has no doubt Cordoba
will testify that Fuhrman was a racist who had called
him "Boy."

Outside of court

• Max Cordoba, appearing in an NBC-TV interview, said he has never spoken with F. Lee Bailey.

Wednesday
March 15, 1995
64th day of sequestration
Jury not present

• The cross-examination of Detective Mark Fuhrman by F. Lee Bailey was delayed today while Bailey
underwent a blistering attack by Marcia Clark. Bailey
had stated in court yesterday that he had personally
spoken to prospective defense witness Max Cordoba,
"Marine to Marine." He told Judge Ito, "I haven't the
slightest doubt that he'll march up to that witness

stand and tell the world what Fuhrman called him." Cordoba, a Sergeant in the Marines, is an African-American. Marcia Clark told the judge that Bailey had lied to the court yesterday. She bolstered her contention by playing a taped segment from last night's "Dateline" show on NBC. In the interview Max Cordoba denied having spoken with Bailey. Bailey indignantly attempted to explain by saying Cordoba was "confused." Marcia Clark and F. Lee Bailey entered into a heated exchange in which Clark got the better of Bailey, who blustered, became flustered and was told by Judge Ito to sit down and control himself. A red-faced Bailey complied. He had insulted Clark by saying her eyesight and memory were deficient.

• Judge Ito ruled against allowing Max Cordoba to testify until he has been questioned outside the presence of the jury in regard to whether or not he had spoken with F. Lee Bailey.

Jury present

• F. Lee Bailey resumed his cross-examination of Detective Fuhrman, and while it was often loud and sarcastic, it did not appear to score any points for the defense. Bailey at times seemed to be rattled from his earlier dressing down, while Fuhrman maintained his calm composure throughout, denying that he is a racist. Detective Fuhrman is expected to complete his appearance for the prosecution tomorrow.

Thursday
March 16, 1995
65th day of sequestration
Jury not present

• Marcia Clark for the prosecution and F. Lee Bailey for the defense met in Judge Lance Ito's chambers to iron out their differences from yesterday. Clark had called Bailey a liar and backed up her accusation with caught-on-tape video evidence. Bailey blasted Clark, impugning her eyesight and memory. Judge Ito apparently suggested they apologize on the record, which they did.

• Judge Ito established and disbursed a list of seven rules that the attorneys for both sides are expected to follow henceforth. It was presented in the form of an official court order and as part of the record.

Jury present

• Detective Mark Fuhrman concluded his sixth day as a witness for the prosecution. F. Lee Bailey hoped to make a case that Fuhrman is a racist and had framed O.J. Simpson because he is African-American. He presented no evidence to substantiate that premise, but he plans to call Fuhrman during the defense case.

• L.A.P.D. Lieutenant Frank Spangler, commanding officer at the West Los Angeles division on June

13, was next to testify. He declared that he, or another police officer, was with Detective Fuhrman almost all the time at the Bundy crime scene. He said that no officer ever mentioned seeing more than one glove at Bundy.

• Darryl Smith was sworn next. Smith is a freelance cameraman who was working for "Inside Edition" on June 13. He testified that the video he took of police officers at the crime scene was shot after the area had been released by the police.

• Detective Phillip Vannatter, under questioning by prosecutor Christopher Darden, said it was his idea to have Detective Fuhrman go over the wall of the O.J. Simpson property. He will be on the stand tomorrow to resume testifying.

Outside the court

• Robert Shapiro stunned the media members outside court when he announced his personal disagreement with other members of the defense team over the race issue. He said he felt that race should not be an issue in this case. Other members of the team hastened to claim there is no rift in the defense ranks.

Friday
March 17, 1995
66th day of sequestration

Jury present

• The morning session of the O.J. Simpson trial was delayed for an hour and a half due to another bomb scare.

• Another juror was terminated at 9:30 A.M. A fifty-two-year-old white male Amtrak employee from Glendale was dismissed by Judge Lance Ito for "abundant good cause," though the precise reasons were not given. He was replaced by a sixty-year-old white female, a retired gas company employee.

• Detective Phil Vannatter resumed his testimony under the questioning of Christopher Darden, who elicited the steps taken by the investigator in analyzing the crime scene and evidence present on the site.

• Utilizing charts, the veteran detective described the trail of blood drops which led from O.J. Simpson's Bronco, up the driveway, and into his house. Vannatter's testimony is expected to continue Monday, with cross-examination by Robert Shapiro.

28

Summoned

Tracy

March 16, 1995

"Number 602!"

It was one of the overseers hollering, his voice booming in the small jury room. "Judge Ito wants to see you in his chambers."

I felt a jolt of adrenaline race through me. I had no idea what this could be about. The thing with the maps had been over long ago. What now?

As I folded the cut-to-pieces newspaper I had been reading, others in the jury room turned to look at me. Some tried to read my eyes, trying to see what was going on in my mind. Each one of us knew what it could mean to be summoned to Judge Ito's chambers. We'd seen it happen before. Juror Number 228. Number 320. Number 2017. Number 620. Each, in turn, called to the judge's chambers, then banished, never again to sit in judgment of O.J. Simpson.

I thought I sensed in the looks of some of the jurors a hint of—could it be?—pleasure at my summons. Yes, that was a look of triumph in their eyes. What was that about? I felt awkward, ashamed, embarrassed, and angry. I simply could not figure out why the judge wanted to see me. I hadn't done anything wrong. Or, to be precise, I didn't think I had. Had I?

The deputy who had hollered for me led me down the back hallway in the courthouse to Judge Ito's chambers. Waiting for me there were the judge and the lawyers and, again, the beefy security guys.

No one said hello. No one spoke.

Uh-oh, I thought. This was serious. Again. It was hard to escape the thought that I was suddenly the one on trial.

"Good morning, Number 602," the judge said. "Have a seat, please."

I sat down. "Good morning."

"Number 602," said Judge Ito, his eyes locked into mine, "the reason I've asked you in here, we've had other issues come up that I need to ask you some questions on. And before I do, I want to remind you that you're under oath, the oath that you gave to us or took when you agreed to answer questions regarding your qualifications to serve as a juror."

The stenographer was in the room again, and the

machine made its clickety-clack sounds. Why was
the judge reminding me that I had taken an oath?
That was not a good sign. I searched my mind, furiously trying to think of what could have prompted
this session. Wait. Slow down. The judge needed a
response to his reminder about the oath.

"Yes, sir."

"It has been reported to me," Judge Ito said, "that
you have compiled a list of the names of the jurors in
this case. Is that true?"

The only list I'd ever had was one made up when
we were first sequestered. It was a copy of a list made
up by Catherine Murdoch, one of the first few jurors
excused from the case, who had made up her own
version when we were all just getting to know one
another. After everyone had made introductions, she
made a list of everyone's number and first name and
what they had said they wanted to be called, a nickname or whatever. Her list was incomplete, so I had
volunteered when she had shown it to me to fill in
the blanks. I've always been bad with names. I have
a hard time remembering them. It takes me a long
time even to remember the names of the people I
work with, so I'm in the habit of jotting down names,
and I thought Catherine's list would be a great way
for me to learn the names of the other jurors. She
and I had conducted this conversation in a hallway
in front of other people; we certainly weren't trying
to hide anything from anyone. Later on, I went back
to Catherine with a complete list; it was still mostly
in her handwriting, but I'd filled in the few things
she was missing. To my surprise, she had started a

new list of her own on another scrap of paper. She told me to keep the original scrap, and she would just fill in what was missing on her new page. We compared notes and that was that.

"I didn't compile them," I told the judge, "but I have a list of . . . I have some names of the jurors."

"Why have you done that?" Judge Ito asked.

"No reason. A lady that had the list gave it to me and she said, 'Are these names right?'"

"Who gave the list to you?"

"I don't remember her number. She's gone now."

"Was she one of the jurors who has previously been dismissed?"

"That's correct."

"This wasn't your list, this was something somebody showed to you?"

"That's correct."

"All right," the judge said. He paused, then launched into a new topic.

"It's been reported to me that . . . I have talked to three of the bailiffs, and you have indicated to them that you were writing a book on the case. Is that correct?"

"No. I said I was thinking about it."

"All right. You indicated to them that . . . you've asked them to keep journals in this case or keep a log of events?"

"I don't . . . I said that . . . that I was thinking about doing that, but . . ."

"All right. Did you make mention to them that the newspaper, the *Daily Journal*, was going to assist you in writing a book on this case?" The judge was referring to a widely respected Los Angeles newspaper that covers the courts for lawyers and judges.

"The *Daily Journal*?" I asked.

"*Daily Journal*."

"No, sir. I haven't really made up my mind yet and I certainly haven't talked to anyone about it except just in passing. I think it would be interesting to write a book about it."

"Uh-huh." Another pause. "I've received complaints from a number of jurors that you have taken an unusual interest in the conjugal visit list, that you have made—gone out of your way to examine that list and to get from that list the names of the visitors."

"No, sir, that's not true."

"It's been reported to me that on one occasion regarding one visitation period, that you examined the visitation list on four occasions."

"No, sir."

"Do you know of any reason why you would need to look at that list more than once?"

"No." I thought for a moment, then said, "Well, yes, sir. I think I did look at it twice on one occasion to make sure that my wife was on there."

"All right. Do you recall when we started this case, the day after you were sequestered, you asked the court for permission to use a personal notebook computer?"

"Yes, sir."

"Is there any information on that computer that relates to this case?"

There was not, and I said so: "No, sir, I signed an affidavit to that effect."

"Would you have any objection to my having another judge take your computer and check the database and make sure there's nothing there?"

"Not at all."

"All right. OK."

"The only thing I use that for is to play chess and to run my CD-ROM, which right now, I sent back with my wife because it crashed."

"Are there any necessary passwords?"

"Yes, sir."

"What are those?"

I told him.

"All right," Judge Ito said, adding, "not too tough to figure that one out."

The judge turned to the lawyers. "Mr. Cochran, any comments, questions?"

"Not at this point, Your Honor," Johnnie Cochran said.

"Miss Clark?"

"No," she said.

"All right," the judge said, then turned back to me. "Number 602, do you have anything you want to say about any of these things? You know the procedure we're going through."

"Yes, sir."

"Because of this complaint."

"Pardon me?"

"We've been through this one complaint, or one issue, before. So you understand that I have to look into each one of these things."

"Yes, sir. And I appreciate you doing that because I want to be as truthful and straightforward as possible. There have been some people that asked me about my wife's age, which I didn't think was a big deal, but they had indicated among themselves that they had checked either the phone list or the visitation list to get my wife's age. And if anyone is checking a list, there are people doing it because they aren't . . ."

I stopped, regrouped, then started again. "And I complained a couple times that a deputy sitting over at another table said, 'Who are you calling?' And I had it on a piece of paper, and I said, 'I would like to keep this secret between us.' And he said, 'Oh, yeah, I guess you're right.' "

I wasn't sure that made sense. "So the lists are readily available for everyone to see." There, that was it. "I would like to remain completely anonymous in this case and I'm trying my best to do that, but there are people that look at the list. And a comment was made at the dinner table about my wife's age. She's very sensitive about her age, and I try to be polite without saying, 'It's none of your business.' So all I said was, 'Well, she's older than me,' and someone made the comment, 'Well, she couldn't be because I saw the list.' "

"Who made that comment to you?" Judge Ito asked.

"One of the ladies." I looked around the room. I was thirsty. "My mouth is awfully dry," I said. "One of the ladies at the table. I think it was either 353 or the blonde, the elderly blonde. I don't know her name."

"Elderly blonde," the judge said. "OK."

"You had her in here yesterday, I think."

Mr. Cochran spoke up. "May we approach, Your Honor?"

"Sure," the judge said.

Johnnie Cochran and Marcia Clark walked to the judge's desk and huddled in a sort of mini-sidebar, their voices too low to hear. After a minute or so, they broke up and the judge asked me: "This jury name list, you indicated one of the jurors who has since departed showed you this list?"

"Yes," I said.

"And where was this?"

"She had it—I think it was the lineup for us to come to a meal or something. When we lined up in the hallway, she said, 'Are these names right?' And my name happens to be the same as someone else on the jury, and I said, 'I wish you would scratch that out and just put these initials there because I don't want my name on any list.' "

"So you never had any list of the jurors in your possession, it was just shown to you?"

I hadn't even looked at my list, on a piece of lined notebook paper, in weeks. Early on, I had taken to filing it away in the box containing my floppy disks, which I kept in the black suitcase I used for my computer. That black case was in my room, closed and latched. But I could have sworn I'd thrown the list away weeks ago.

"She gave it to me to correct it and I gave it back

to her. I told her, I said, 'I don't think you should have that.' "

"What was the name of the juror? I mean, do you remember which one it was?"

"Juror 2017 was her name. I don't know anyone's last name, but the jurors call each other by name."

"By first name."

"I have a hard time remembering names."

"OK." The judge looked right at me. "All right. Number 602, as before, I'm going to order you not to discuss what we've discussed here with any of the other jurors. All right?"

"Yes, sir."

"All right. Thank you, sir."

"Thank you."

On the way back down the hall, I played the conversation back again in my mind. I didn't know why I said I hadn't "made up my mind yet" about writing a book. That just popped out without me even thinking. I was not planning to write a book.

Even though I had no such plans, I thought, it sure "would be interesting" to do a book, just as I had told the judge. That reminded me of a conversation I'd had with one of the deputies. He seemed like one of the good guys. He used to take me out running on the patio. That meant he had to be up and ready to run shortly after five in the morning, but he was an early-morning guy like me, so we would jog together on the patio. One morning we were out there, and I said, "Wouldn't this make a hell of a movie?" I was just making idle chatter.

"You're right, it would," he said. Idle chatter back.

"You know," I said, "if you would keep a personal diary of all the things that went on around this trial, you're in the know about a lot more things than I am, I bet you'd have some great stuff by the end of this thing. Then if I kept a diary, I could have my own view. And then if someone else on the outside kept a diary, like that guy in the gallery who's always wearing a jacket and tie and has those glasses and is constantly watching every move we make in the jury box. He watches us like a hawk and he's forever writing things down." I was thinking of Dominick Dunne, the correspondent for *Vanity Fair* magazine, but at the time did not know his name. "After this thing is over, when it's all over and done with, and we're free to say what we want or do whatever want, don't you think this would make a heck of a book? Hey, it might make a heck of a movie."

"Are you kidding me?" the deputy said. "You know what they'd do to me if I was keeping a diary?"

"What would be wrong with you keeping a diary?" I asked. "I'm keeping a diary."

That drew no response.

Maybe, I thought as I made my way back to the jury room, the deputy wasn't such a good guy after all. Maybe he ratted me out to the judge. I hadn't told any other deputies about my diary. I certainly hadn't suggested to any of the other deputies that they keep a journal. I had no idea why Judge Ito thought I had told three deputies to keep journals. I had spoken about the issue with one deputy, and that conversation was just talk while we were jogging. Perhaps it had been taken as a violation of the rules and I'd been reported.

Then there was this thing about me checking out the conjugal visit lists. Where did that come from? That list was maintained by a female deputy with whom I'd had words. Maybe this was a way for her to cause trouble for me. Though it was vitally important to me each week that Judy be on that list, the actual act of putting her name on the form was a task that I would take care of, then almost immediately forget that I'd accomplished it. In my worry, I'd felt compelled to go back and check. But I assuredly was not checking up on anyone else's visitors. What did I care who was visiting who? I didn't.

So, bottom line, I said to myself: I had a list. That was what I'd really been called in to chambers to talk about. But I'd been open and aboveboard about it. I'd told the absolute truth. Was a list worse than having maps?

There was no denying that I'd had such a list. Why would that matter anymore? The list had long since served its purpose. It certainly wouldn't matter at all if I'd thrown it out. The thing was, I just couldn't be positive that I'd tossed it. I thought I had, but . . .

If I hadn't, I could see that it could become a big problem. It shouldn't, but I could see how it could. The jury was supposed to be anonymous—no one knew that better than me. Someone could see that list and think that it had been designed to reveal the names of those on the jury. It hadn't been written for

that reason, of course, but that was a possible inter-
pretation. In my mind, we were still anonymous to
the outside world. The list was not for anyone on the
outside. It was for use on the inside.

I walked back into the jury room. No one spoke to
me. No one was under any illusions about what a
summons to Judge Ito's chambers could mean. We'd
all seen it before. The others knew that if my visit to
the judge's chambers had been for some minor matter, I would have said something, anything, to brush
it off, to let them know it was no big deal. But I could
say nothing. So they sensed—no, they knew with a
certainty—that I was on the hook, waiting to be
called again.

After a few moments passed, a few of the jurors
looked at me. Francine, Farron, Number 19; and
Number 1290. These were the same ones who'd
taken such pleasure in my earlier trip to the judge's
chambers. Now they were looking especially pleased.

I was dangling. I was all by myself. With no one to
talk to. No one to reach out to and no one reaching
out to me.

It was odd. I'd been locked up with all these people
for over two months, and no one had even an ounce
of empathy or was willing to register any understanding. I didn't get it. And what exactly were all
those pleased looks about? Had all four of them been
in to see the judge? If they had, what had they said?
Given the frosty way I was getting along with that
group, they could have said anything. If they'd each
been in to see him, that meant that someone had to
have written the judge a letter complaining about

me. What could it have said? How long had he had the note? How many people had signed it?

Here I was, confronted with an investigation, wondering whether I was going to be thrown off the most famous jury in the history of the country, facing what seemed like certain public humiliation if I was dismissed, and the people with whom I'd been living were either cold as ice or barely containing their joy at the thought of me being in trouble. It was awful.

✳

When we went back to the hotel that night, I noticed that my computer was gone, all my disks were gone, even the black case was gone. And whatever had been in the case was also gone, seized by the deputies.

I had stashed the diary that Judy had prompted me to keep inside a drawer in the room. It was gone, too.

Not once had I thought of that diary as the stuff of a book. But when I saw that all of my stuff was missing, the thought hit me: That diary is probably something that would not make anyone's approved list.

"Up at four or five," a typical entry might start. "Ran for twenty minutes. Brought fruit for breakfast. Went to work on time. From courtroom came home. Had second helping for lunch. Court ended early. Really enjoyed the movie."

I did sometimes write impressions of things I saw in the courtroom. One day, Marcia Clark was having a really bad day, it seemed to me. Everything she did or said seemed just wrong. The defense was loving it. They knew it, they could feel it, they were champing at the bit to take advantage of it. So that day I wrote something in there about that.

More often, though, I wrote about how I was feeling, like, "I'm feeling trapped in this hotel." Or, when Farron made the issue of me picking my teeth at the dinner table, I wrote about how that episode had hurt my feelings.

It was that sort of thing. It was not an analysis of the evidence. It was not about O.J. Simpson's guilt or innocence. It wasn't often about the lawyers. Or even about Judge Ito. It most certainly wasn't a book. It was just me, alone with a notebook and my feelings, glad for some place to vent the frustrations and hardships of being locked up. At first I'd resisted it. I'm not a writer. I don't even like writing letters. But as the weeks wore on, Judy proved to be right. I found that the notebook was the one place I could release the pressure I was feeling and let a bit of steam escape from the boiling pot.

After a while, I really got into it. It felt really good to write out my feelings. If I had torn the pages out of the notebook and thrown them away, I think it would have served the same purpose. But I didn't. I never used the computer; I had signed an affidavit saying I would not use it to take notes, and I honored that vow. And though the notebook was Judy's idea, I never showed it to her. She would just ask, "Are you writing things down?" I'd answer yes, and that was it. We didn't discuss it beyond that.

Nevertheless, a feeling of dread crept over me. If I

was confronted with the undeniable existence of the notebook, how would I make anyone understand that keeping a diary was an innocent thing? I'd given my vow to carry out my duties as a juror to the best of my abilities. Not for one second had I ever had any intent to break that vow.

That night I tossed and turned, unable to clear my mind of either the diary or the list. I was worried. I hardly slept. Trouble was about—bad trouble for me. I didn't know why. But I knew.

✳

Later I learned that I had good reason to wonder about the jurors who'd shot me such looks of pleasure when I returned to the jury room.

Judge Ito eventually released transcripts revealing that several jurors had written him a note complaining about me. He interviewed them, then interviewed me.

Who complained about me? Francine, Farron, Number 1290 and Number 19. To say that each of them had an interest in seeing me off the jury, I think, would be an understatement.

Number 19 and I were not on speaking terms.

At least he was a member of the regular jury. Number 1290 was an alternate. Farron was an alternate (and would remain one until May 1, when she replaced Tracy Hampton). Francine had been an alternate until March 1, when she took Michael Knox's place. Each of the alternates always wanted to be on the regular jury. That was just human nature.

It was Number 19 who told the judge about the list. He said he'd seen me with it. Farron also said Number 19 had told her he'd seen me with the list.

Some of the other complaints were particularly petty. Some were just plain cheap shots.

Number 1290 said I put my feet up on the furniture and gargled at the dinner table.

Farron said I had a Walkman and headphones on at the dinner table. But "another juror," she said, "pointed out to me there's no cassette in that Walkman." She suggested the Walkman allowed me to play eavesdropper. What I had was not a cassette player but a portable CD player. And it would have been virtually impossible to see what was inside the player because I kept it in a front pocket in my sweatsuit. In truth, I did have a CD in it and the player was on. I was listening to the classical guitar CD that Leona Boyd had left for me after her visit.

Number 19 and Number 1290 each said there had been occasions when I'd ridden in a van by myself to or from the courthouse. "Nobody wants to be around him," Number 19 said. The fact was, I rode by myself exactly one time. Leaving the hotel one morning, I was the last one out; everyone else was crammed into two vans, so I got in the third. When we got to the courthouse, one of the ladies on the jury said with a tone of envy, "Did you get to ride in that van all by yourself?" She and two other jurors rode back with me in the same van.

I wasn't being avoided. In fact, after interviewing Farron, Francine, Number 19, and Number 1290,

Judge Ito interviewed Number 2179. She wasn't in their clique, and she said, "I don't have a problem with 602."

Later, Farron and Francine were both kicked off.

29

✧

Excused

Tracy

March 17, 1995

The next morning, the deputy called for me again.

"602!"

When my number rang out again in the jury room, it seemed as if my heart stopped. Everything slowed way down. Things didn't seem real.

Approaching the judge's chambers, my mouth was dry. I needed water. I was really scared.

I reminded myself as I made my way down the hall of the many times I had thought of how I'd been drafted to do a job, been called to civic duty, and how badly I'd wanted to do a good job. I'd given of myself emotionally, tried to do the best I could, hadn't formed an opinion about O.J. Simpson's guilt or innocence, had thought I'd abided by the rules, had played it fair and square.

This may sound silly, but I also remembered as I walked down that hall that my wife had left town Thursday on a business trip. She had gone to Las Vegas for a couple of days and I knew that if anything was going to happen, it would be while Judy was out of town. Unreachable. Unavailable.

In Judge Ito's chambers, the mood was once again all business. Marcia Clark, Christopher Darden, Johnnie Cochran, and the other members of the Dream Team—everyone was solemn.

"602, have a seat, please," Judge Ito said.

I sat down.

"602, when I looked in your computer, in the floppy disk box there's a list which appears to have names of jurors."

"You're right," I said, feeling a crushing sense of regret and embarrassment. "I thought I threw it away."

"All right," Judge Ito said.

He paused. Later I learned that he had already told the lawyers in the case more about his discovery. Right before I'd been called to his chambers that morning, he had told the attorneys about the list: names and jury numbers on a piece of ruled notebook paper about four inches by six inches. This discovery, he told the attorneys, was "directly contrary" to what

I'd told him the day before, that I did not have such a list and had only been shown one.

"Number 602," Judge Ito said, "I'm going to discharge you as a member of this jury. I'm going to order you not to reveal to anybody the identity of any member of the jury or any of the alternates. I am going to order you not to reveal to anyone the name or location of the facility where the jurors are sequestered.

"I'm going to admonish you, pursuant to Penal Code section 116.5, that it is a violation of the law to accept or agree to accept any payment or benefit in consideration for supplying any information in relation to this case prior to or within 90 days of the discharge of the jury.

"I'm also going to warn you that it appears that the statement you made to me yesterday on your oath as a juror was not correct and I may be referring this matter to another agency to investigate.

"All right. You are discharged, sir.

"Let me give you a copy of the order so you understand it clearly."

It felt like the world came crashing down. The court, the prosecution and defense, the judge, O.J. Simpson, the victims, the victims' families. I felt I had let down so many people. I knew that both sides and the judge had worked really hard, that we had spent a bundle of taxpayer money, my money, on this, and I had just let everyone down. Most of all, I had let myself down. I had been called to judge and instead had myself been judged a failure.

I stood up. I'll never forget this because I wanted

to say something to everyone in that room and I could barely speak. I wanted to apologize to everybody, to each person in the room individually. I was really sorry. I wanted to tell them that I didn't mean to do anything wrong.

"I apologize to everyone," I said.

I wanted to say more. But no words came out.

Standing there, I got the feeling I was being given the bum's rush and they were throwing me out.

I turned around and slowly walked out.

After I left the judge's chambers, I found out later, Judge Ito called out after me, "Have a nice day." Was he being sarcastic? Snide? To this day, I don't know. He also mentioned that the diary had been found and he wanted to take a look at it.

Outside the door, a deputy shoved the black case in my arms and said, "Here's your computer. That notebook you had has been confiscated and turned over to another department for possible criminal action."

Criminal action? For writing down how I felt? In a daze, I started walking again, down the hall, past the jury room, past the door that held the others. I was now dismissed. A few minutes before, I had been one of them in that room. Abruptly, that was no more. I was not even allowed to peek my head in the door and say good-bye.

I made it to the end of the hall. A female deputy, the one with whom I had sparred, was there. "Well," she said, "we're rid of you." It seemed as if she was particularly enjoying a moment of revenge, savoring a delicious moment at my expense.

Other deputies took me back to the hotel. A sergeant said, "Go get your stuff together. We've got five minutes or ten minutes, something like that. Get your stuff together and we'll take you home."

I was devastated and feeling lower and lower still as time ticked by.

My room held an amazing amount of stuff. I naturally had more stuff than I had arrived with, more than I could pack, because Judy had been bringing me things. Like a zombie, I started throwing everything into plastic bags.

I got one of those carts you move luggage around on and put my things on it, then wheeled it to the Control Point. No one offered to help.

At the Control Point, a sergeant said, "Those bags have the hotel name on them. I can't let you take them."

I was really out of it. I hadn't even thought of that. "Oh, you're right. I forgot."

He gave me one of those industrial-strength garbage bags, the huge kind, and I emptied all the stuff in the smaller bags into it, then set it among the suitcases on the cart.

"Are you ready yet?" the sergeant asked as I was struggling with this chore.

"No."

A couple of minutes later: "Well, are you finally ready?"

"Yes."

We rode down the elevator to the basement, where

they put me and my suitcases and that big plastic bag in a white patrol car. I got in the back seat and we left.

The deputies in front asked me for our address and directions to the condo. I said they could follow this street and that one and a particular freeway, but they paid no attention. Instead, one of them said, "When we get close, you can tell us the way." It seemed to me that this was their final slap in the face. They wanted me to know they weren't going to listen to my directions until we got close to our home—that they knew all things better than I did, even how to get to my house.

I don't know if that was intentional or not. But it certainly felt demeaning.

As we neared the house, the deputies said the media would probably be there. I said that was nonsense, that no one knew where I lived. Judy and I had gone to such lengths to ensure our anonymity.

We came up the street and I saw a lot of vans, news vans. I thought, how in the world did they find out?

I asked the deputies to take me through the gates and to a back elevator. They did, but the news crews found me. These people just came at me in hordes. Microphones and cameras and lights and everyone shouting. What I wanted to do at that point was crawl in a hole and die because I'd let so many people down.

The reporters kept asking, "How do you feel? How do you feel?"

"Devastated," was all I could say.

✦

Until that point in my life, I'd had very little experience with newspeople. That night I gained a lot of respect for them.

Of course I didn't have a key to the condominium. Thankfully, Judy had left a spare key where I would know to look. I fished it out and had just inserted it into the lock when someone came up and said, "Are you . . ."

"No," I said.

"Yes, you are. I've seen you in court."

"OK, I am."

"Listen," this person said. "I know that right now is not a good time. I don't want to cause you any problems. Here is my card."

This was Avi Cohen, a producer for CBS News. I was touched. He was being so gracious. "Why don't you come in?" I said.

Other reporters and producers introduced themselves. And we sat and talked. We sat from about one in the afternoon until about five-thirty, when Judy arrived home. I did most of the talking. The newspeople sat on the golden-colored sofa, and I sat across the room by the fireplace. At the outset, I demanded that whatever I said be kept off the record. To their credit, each one of the producers and reporters in that room promised that it would never be printed or aired, and each one kept that promise. These were good people from the press. I talked and they listened. Avi Cohen from CBS, Stacie Griffith from NBC's "Today" show, Tracie Savage from KNBC Channel 4 in Los Angeles, Randy Paige and Stephanie Medina Rodriguez from KCAL Channel 9, Dana Wolfe from ABC's "Nightline," and Dree DeClamecy from CNN—they all just sat and listened.

The crews lurking downstairs, however, insisted on some sort of statement for the evening broadcasts. So I wrote something and Dree DeClamecy ran downstairs and read it to the waiting hordes. "There was no personal conflict, no physical confrontation, no race problem, no money offered or accepted," the statement said. Referring to me in the third person, she went on with the statement: "He was notified at 9:30 A.M. that he was being excused from the jury. He describes himself as devastated and overwhelmed, but glad to be home, glad to be out of the situation and glad to be able to go on with his life, as normal as it can be. And, finally, he is not at all comfortable with media attention." When she came back upstairs, after reading my statement, she said, "They want more and they won't leave until they get more."

So the people upstairs pooled their resources and shot tape of me answering some questions.

The newspeople stayed a long time, so long that they ordered pizza delivered to the condo and we all wolfed it down. By then I was finally talked out. They were just about to leave when Judy arrived. She came in and the TV lights went on. We hugged. We were just about in tears, both of us, and this feeling of relief and safety and gratitude enveloped me as soon as she held me.

As she held me, she knew, she could tell instantly, that I was down—terribly, awfully, horribly down. Lower than I had ever been.

30

✧

Pandemonium

Judy

March 17–19, 1995

I will never forget driving up the hill to our condo that Friday afternoon. It looked as if Camp O.J. had moved to Glendale.

Satellite trucks were parked everywhere. Lights and cameras had been planted on the ground, and wires snaked every which way. People were standing in the street, gesturing frantically and yelling at each other about who knows what. I thought, I must get control of this; I don't want them to get to Tracy.

I'd just gotten off the plane from Las Vegas, where I'd been on business. I figured that Tracy and I had taken such care in hiding our address, that even the sheriff's deputies couldn't find us, and so I was expecting it would be just the two of us, Tracy and me, and we would finally have some time together alone.

I parked the car. As I got out, I saw Stan Chambers, one of the most respected TV reporters in Los Angeles. Then I saw Linda Deutsch, the esteemed Associated Press reporter who specializes in covering court trials. "Everybody's upstairs in your unit," Linda said. Upstairs? How could that be? She hopped into the elevator to let Tracy and the others know I was on my way.

I looked over and saw a TV reporter interviewing a neighbor. Craziness. I got off the elevator, carrying my luggage and ran into the building maintenance manager. He pointed to our unit like, surprise, surprise. I opened the door and as I did, an incredible battery of blinding lights went on and Tracy came to the door and hugged me.

I was so glad to see him.

Everybody started introducing themselves. Avi Cohen said he'd been there since noon. "It was a very unique experience for me," he said. "I was able to have on not just my journalist hat but to put on my therapist hat, too. It was a special experience." I will be forever grateful to the reporters and producers who were there with Tracy that afternoon; they saw the pain he was in and did not take advantage of his vulnerability.

The pandemonium carried on for some time, moving well into the evening. Avi was the last to go. When he left, Tracy and I just sort of sat there.

❧

The next couple days flew by. We barely slept. We barely ate. The phone never stopped ringing.

We were truly amazed that so many reporters and producers wanted to talk to us. Bryant Gumbel, Larry King, Harry Smith, Bill Ritter. With rare exception, though, the questions did not reach the depth of Tracy's experience. He'd be asked, "What did you think about the prosecution?" Or, "Is the Dream Team all it's cracked up to be?" We tried desperately to focus the interviews on the emotional and psychological turmoil he'd been through, but to no avail.

After a few interviews, I realized that our effort was bound to be futile because the press had no idea about what it was truly like on the inside. The public perception was one of a luxury hotel, free and unlimited food, private concerts, and no worries about L.A. traffic—a maximum vacation with five dollars salary per day to boot.

I decided I needed to push. I began to wear a butterfly pin, and I'd tell anyone who would listen that the butterfly was a symbol; it starts out as an ugly caterpillar but then changes into a beautiful thing, one able to take flight in a new direction. That was what Tracy and I hoped would happen to the jury system if we could get people to take a good look at its shortcomings.

During the interviews, Tracy and I would hold hands. It wasn't a conscious thing. It just happened, and I would briefly feel that connection we'd always had. But on the way home, I noticed that he would get very, very quiet and it was painful to see the blankness in his eyes.

278

31

🦅

A Kiss Good-bye

Tracy

March–May, 1995

The whirlwind of inter-
views lasted just a few days. When it ended, it was as
if the reality in which I'd been immersed for so long
had suddenly evaporated, leaving me adrift without
structure or context to my life. At the same time,
each reminder of the trial proved painful. It was a
contradiction that made no sense.

A couple of days after I was dismissed, Judy and I
went to a grocery store. It felt odd to be out in public
without the overseers. I expected someone to order
me back in line. I felt overwhelmed by the choices

confronting me. Were there really three dozen different kinds of yogurt? My eyes swept up and down the aisles, looking over everyone and each display. Were people looking at me? I was not sure. Did they recognize me? I did not know. If they did, what were they thinking? I could only guess.

The Tuesday after I was dismissed was Judy's birthday. We went to a party at her office. Every time someone would ask me about the case, I felt myself get tense. I could feel a tightness in my stomach and my mind flashed on the bloody pictures of Nicole Brown Simpson and Ron Goldman. I could not help myself. There were the bodies. The blood. Right in front of me.

Trying to clear my head, I would go for walks around the neighborhood. One day, a sheriff's department patrol car flashed by on the street. I thought, they're after me.

Another day, one of the sheriff's buses drove by. The driver honked at somebody. I was sure he was honking at me, telling me it was time to get on the bus.

Judy told me I was being too hard on myself. She said I was blaming myself fiercely. Let it go, she said.

Two weeks after I was excused from the jury, I went back to work. Amtrak was in transition. I was thankful I still had a job but found I answered to a new boss. It was like starting a new job, and that in and of itself is stressful. I thought perhaps I could find familiar comfort in the job itself—after all, an air conditioner is an air conditioner. But it's not. There were new parts, new equipment with which I had to become familiar. And while I was teaching, I felt as if everyone was watching me, judging me and finding me wanting, waiting for me to misidentify an air conditioning part or miss a repair procedure, waiting for me to fail. I felt I couldn't do anything right.

Often, I would come home from work and tell Judy, "I just dread going back. I don't think I can handle it."

"You'll get through it," she'd tell me. "It'll be OK."

It wasn't OK. It seemed that two or three people would mention the trial each day at work. Someone would ask, "What's going on with O.J.?" I'd say, "I'm not keeping up with it. I don't care." The name Rosa Lopez came up frequently. I'd say that none of her testimony took place in front of the jury. I wasn't believed. "Were you asleep that day or something? I saw her on the stand. They were questioning her and Judge Ito was right beside her on the bench." I'd say, "You don't understand. The jury wasn't there for that."

Each time the trial was mentioned at work, my stomach would knot up. I'd get so I couldn't talk. Sometimes I could feel tears well up in my eyes and I would have to walk away.

I had no appetite. I lost weight.

I couldn't sleep. I'd toss and turn. In the middle of the night, I'd lie awake in the darkness and stare at the ceiling.

One day in May, Judy and I were in the kitchen of the condo. She was standing between me and the doorway. It was as if there was no way out. I felt a rushing sense of panic, and I bolted past her, out onto the balcony. I stood there with my hands on the rail. It was all I could do to breathe.

"Are you OK?" Judy asked.

I put up my hand, to say, back off, give me some room.

A few minutes later, I went back inside. I tried to explain. I had just gotten a drink of water. When I turned around, I discovered that she had opened a door to one of the kitchen cabinets. She was blocking my way out. The door was blocking my way out. I felt confined, cornered in a very narrow space. My mouth became dry. I couldn't breathe. I had to get out of there.

After that episode I started to think about my options. The only one that seemed like a real solution was to kill myself. What was there to go on for? I was tired of everything. Worn out. No good. I didn't want to be a burden to Judy any longer, didn't want to hurt her anymore.

"Please," Judy said, unaware I was considering suicide. "Go see Bruce." Bruce Weimer, the neurologist.

That afternoon, after my appointment with Bruce, I came home to find the jury summons. That night, I told Judy of my plans. She asked me to take the medicine Bruce had prescribed, to give myself some time, to give us the gift of time.

The next day, Saturday, May 27, was a delightful day. We spent it in each other's arms. Still, I could not shake the overwhelming feeling of failure. I could not deal with it. I simply could not. That night I could not sleep. I looked at my wife and thought, I cannot do this to her anymore. So I got up and took all the prescription pills I could find. I'd read somewhere that you weren't supposed to mix drugs with alcohol; I found a bottle of cooking wine in the refrigerator and, for good measure, finished it off. I walked through the house and took a good look around. I figured I wasn't going to be seeing any of it anymore.

Then I got into bed and kissed my wife good-bye.

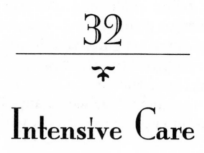

32

Intensive Care

Judy

May 28–June 2, 1995

I woke up about five-thirty in the morning. I heard Tracy sleeping. He was breathing deeply and I thought, thank goodness, he's finally gotten a good night's sleep. If I move, I thought, he'll wake up. So I lay there next to him for about two hours. He seemed to be in the deepest of sleeps.

At seven-thirty, I slipped out of bed, figuring he was sleeping so deeply that I could ease out of the room. This seemed to be the first decent sleep he'd had in months. I was delighted. I put on a warm-up suit and got the paper. The coffee had been on the timer, so I relaxed with a cup and the morning news. Usually, I would also take a Xanax tablet, my migraine therapy, but the bottle was still in the bedroom, and I hadn't wanted to rattle it around for fear I would wake up Tracy.

At eight-fifteen, I tiptoed back into the bedroom, looking for the Xanax bottle. I looked over by my bedside table, where I always keep it, and it was gone.

And I knew at that instant exactly what he had done.

I went into his bathroom and found the bottle. He had left three tablets for me. The most bizarre thought came over me: That was so like him to be so thoughtful to leave me three pills.

I looked at every other bottle in the medicine cabinet and everything was empty. Right then, it occurred to me what he'd said: "Don't tell anybody. Promise me you'll forgive me."

I went and sat down in the living room and thought, I can't believe this is happening. I dialed 911 and calmly told them I needed an ambulance. They asked me why. I said, "I think my husband has taken an overdose of pills and tried to kill himself." The operator asked me to check if Tracy was still breathing. He was. She asked me to check his pulse. It was weak. She told me to roll him over onto his left side and said paramedics were on the way.

While they were en route, I searched the condo for a suicide note. I searched all the usual places we leave each other notes but could find nothing. Finally I checked the ditty bag Tracy used to take with him to court. There it was. It said he could not go on. In the last six months he'd begun to feel he could go on no more. So many things had happened and he didn't want the way he was feeling to affect our relationship. He loved me more than anything in the world and this was the only way he could see out. He signed it, "I love you."

It took just a few minutes for the paramedics to arrive. With them was a policeman who'd known the address because he'd been here the day Tracy was released from the jury.

As the paramedics worked on Tracy, the policeman led me into the living room. He had some questions, he said, but I knew he was trying to shield me from the scene in the bedroom. The officer took down the usual data. As he finished, the paramedics came out and announced they were taking Tracy to the closest hospital in Verdugo Hills. They needed to get there quickly.

I followed them in my car. I felt calm. It was as if the entire experience was unfolding before me but happening to someone else. It didn't seem real.

At the emergency room, the paramedics wheeled Tracy back behind closed doors. I filled out forms. The hospital admitted Tracy as "John Doe," not wanting to alert the media, for which I was grateful.

After fifteen or twenty minutes, a doctor came out. He took me down a hall and asked, "Would you like me to call a priest?"

"No," I said. "But thank you."

"Is there anyone you'd like us to call?" My family

was in North Carolina, his in Florida. Our boys were out of town. I didn't want to call anyone, really. What could they do?

I sat in a small room off the emergency entrance. The police officer and one of the paramedics came by and sat with me for a while. One of them said Tracy was "very critical" and offered to sit with me as long as I wanted.

"He's going to be so upset with me," I said. "I had promised I wouldn't tell anyone."

"It's important that you don't blame yourself," the officer said. "You can't feel guilty. You didn't know what he'd done. It's not your fault."

The rational side of my mind knew that, accepted it even. But then another part of me knew, too, that this was something he wanted to do. He felt it was his only way out.

But I couldn't understand why that was so.

Tracy had always told me that suicide is a permanent solution to a temporary problem. Yet when we'd spoken in the Jacuzzi on Friday night, I couldn't get him to grasp this logic. Sitting there in that small room, I became really angry. I was furious that he had not given it a month, at least tried the medication.

I sat in that small room for hours. Behind the closed doors, the doctors pumped Tracy's stomach. They did a CAT scan and all kinds of other tests, looking to see what initial damage the overdose had done and whether any vital organs had been hit beyond repair. About two in the afternoon, one of the nurses appeared at the door. "If you'd like to see him . . ." she said.

As we walked, the nurse warned me that Tracy was not conscious. It would be several days, she said, before he would rally enough for that.

We turned a corner and entered a room, and there he was, virtually lifeless under a sheet. He wore a beautiful gold chain and it had been cut off. A tube had been jammed up his nose. His left arm was shaved from the elbow down. He was surrounded by IV bags and plastic tubes. He was hooked up to the oxygen machine. I saw a catheter.

He was a pathetic, pitiful sight. I reached for his hand. I squeezed it, caressed it. Please be strong, I prayed. I can't let you go. I spoke to him: "I'm not giving you up without a fight. I'm sorry for not doing what I promised, but I just can't let you go."

At some point, one of the doctors entered the room. "Has he ever had any history of this?" the doctor asked.

"Absolutely not."

"Why in the world would he do this?"

"He was on the O.J. jury and it stressed him out."

"I haven't been keeping up at all with that case. Give me some background."

That took some time. "I'm going to keep him in the intensive care unit," the doctor said. "Anytime anyone attempts suicide, we have to keep them under observation for seventy-two hours. But I want to tell you: He's going to be here longer than that. There's so much poison in his system that it will be several days."

The rest of the day was a blur. A couple times, Tracy opened his eyes. I told him then that I loved him. He would close his eyes. No acknowledgment. No response.

Day turned to night. One of the nurses finally slipped into the room and said to me, "You've had a really long day. Why don't you go home and try to get some rest? He's not going to wake up for a while. We'll take good care of him."

I dragged myself home. Physically, I was exhausted. But my mind kept racing. In my head, I kept going over everything that had happened, from Friday night on. I lay there awake in the dark and couldn't stop the fear from washing over me, a fear so raw it made me shiver.

Every hour I called the hospital to see how Tracy was doing. The nurses would say he was resting, not to worry. They'd tell me to try to get some sleep.

But I could not sleep at all.

As dawn neared, I noticed I was feeling lightheaded. I hadn't eaten in about forty-eight hours and, even when things around me are normal, I feel woozy if I haven't eaten regularly.

This can't happen today, I thought. I've got to get to the hospital to be with him.

At six in the morning, when I checked in with one of the nurses, I told her, "I'm really having a tough time. When I get up, I feel as if I'm going to faint. But I know I need to be there."

"You probably ought to get yourself to the emergency room," she said. "Let them know what's up."

On the way over to the hospital, I had to pull over twice to the side of the road and open the car door. I tried to throw up but there was nothing there. The dry heaves. It was painful and terrible and frightened me. The nausea was overwhelming and I felt so lightheaded. I shouldn't have been driving, but I didn't want to call the paramedics again.

I staggered into the ER. They took one look at me and hooked me up to an IV. One bag of solution drained into me, then another. After that, the nurses let me go, with a warning to take care of myself.

Up the stairs I went, to the intensive care unit, to Tracy and the tubes keeping him going. A few times during the day, his eyes fluttered open. I told him then that I loved him. But he still was not conscious and did not respond. Mostly I sat there and cried. I could not hold back the tears, thinking how close I had come to losing my very best friend, the man who'd always been a rock in my life. I thought of what sequestration had done to him, of all the times I had tried to tell someone at the sheriff's department that some sort of intervention session ought to be held, of how I had become so absolutely certain that being sequestered was going to produce a horrible aftermath. I'd never in my wildest dreams, however, imagined that it would hit Tracy so hard. Of all people. He'd always been so strong.

Then I thought: If it could happen to him, it could happen to anyone.

I chewed on that thought as the day passed. All

day long, I sat there by Tracy's side and held his hand. At night, the nurses gently told me to go home and get some sleep. Before I left, I asked the nurses to turn on the television in his room. That way, if by chance he woke up in the middle of the night and he was able to get his senses about him, he would know that he was not being sequestered.

❋

I got a bit of sleep. In the morning, back at the hospital, I tried to look with fresh eyes at my husband. He looked like a very old man. I barely recognized him.

A few hours after I arrived, Tracy opened his eyes. He looked around the room, not really focusing on anything, and whispered, "Why? Why didn't you let me go?"

"I'm sorry," I said to him in a soft voice. "I'm so sorry. But that was non-negotiable. I could not let you go."

Tracy began to cry, then let loose—still in a hoarse whisper—with several choice four-letter words. I reminded him that he had always told me we could do anything together, that it was us against the world. "We're going to beat this," I said. "We'll get through this together."

He slowly shook his head from side to side. I looked at his eyes. They registered complete defeat. "You know," he said, "I'm going to complete this."

Just seconds before I'd been hopeful. Tracy was still alive. With that comment, though, I sank back into despair. Would I have to worry each day that I'd come home from work to find him dead on the sofa? What did this mean for us for the rest of our lives?

Tracy drifted back to unconsciousness. A few more times that day, he woke up. Each time, he insisted, "I want to know exactly what happened. Tell me what happened." I'd go through it, and he'd whisper, "Why? Why didn't you let me go?"

It was agonizing. And as I sat there, I found myself feeling an incandescent anger as well. I was absolutely furious at the justice system and what it had done to him. They isolated him and then they took away his identity, took complete control of his life, took away everything from him that made him unique, that made him Tracy, and they made him into a paranoid, agitated, angry man with no desire to live. That was not fair. They had said sequestration was not going to be a picnic. Well, that severely misstated the situation. In no way did it even come close to explain the extent of the dehumanization. My husband was lying in a hospital bed, hooked up to a bunch of tubes and I didn't know if he would ever be well again, if he would ever work again, what was going to happen in the next few minutes or even the next few days—and it was not right.

Late that afternoon, a doctor came into the room. He said Tracy was in a deep depression, a "black hole," he called it. Tracy interrupted to say, "I don't want to live anymore" and began to cry. After a while, he cried himself to sleep.

That evening the nurses brought Tracy something to eat. He hadn't eaten solid food since Saturday and it was now Tuesday evening but he looked at the tray

and said, "I'm not going to eat." Then he looked at
it again and announced, "I'm going to eat myself to
death." He had no hand-eye coordination, however,
and he couldn't get anything in his mouth. I started
to feed him and he snapped, "Don't baby me. I don't
want to be babied." He reached for the spoon or
where he thought the spoon was and missed. He
tried again and again and kept missing. He got agitated. He resorted to eating with his finger and that
seemed to work better, so he announced again, "I'm
just going to eat the whole thing. I'm going to eat
myself to death." He ate everything on the tray.

After dinner, he looked around a bit at his surroundings, trying to orient himself. I told him he was
in a hospital room. He said he felt he was in a hotel
room again. I showed him the TV, pointed out that it
was on, and I opened the curtains so he could see
outside. "See the differences?" I asked in the most
hopeful tone I could manage. He grunted.

Tracy asked if anyone knew about what had happened. Yes, I said. A few people. Not many.

"Do the nurses know?" he asked. "I don't want
the nurses to know."

"The nurses know. They had to know." That hadn't
occurred to him. He shook his head and fell back
asleep.

On Wednesday morning, Tracy woke up and announced, "Damn. Failed again."

This is his first memory of waking up after the suicide attempt. He had no memory of any our conversations the day before.

That morning, a psychiatrist came round. He said it was likely Tracy would be released from the hospital in forty-eight hours but suggested strongly that he check himself in somewhere where he could receive full-time supervision and some therapy. Tracy's doctor agreed with that recommendation, and so arrangements were made for Tracy to go to Las Encinas Hospital, a private mental health facility in nearby Pasadena. The plan was for him to stay there a full week, then ease back to living at home and going back to work.

That Friday, the transfer was made. He had to be under constant supervision, so I followed in a separate car. When we got there, the psychologist who checked Tracy into Las Encinas recognized him from TV. She told me that when she'd seen Tracy on the tube the night of March 17, she said to herself that he looked like a man who was going to be having some heavy psychological problems. Even on TV, she could just tell.

🦅

The psychologist's name is Kathy, and she and I talked frequently over the following week that Tracy stayed at Las Encinas. Anyone at that hospital, she said, would have given their time to talk with the jury about being dehumanized and isolated. She said they would have been glad to have done it even for free. I said I didn't understand why the legal system had never asked anyone in the psychological community for some help. She said she didn't understand, either.

❦

Las Encinas is an old Spanish-style place, and as we walked in, the first thing Tracy said was, "I'm back in sequestration. I'm back in a hotel."

He checked in as John Doe again, and as the orderlies took his bags away and searched him, he said, "Here we go again." The orderlies tried to be sensitive, but they had to take his Swiss Army knife away from him as well as his belt. As they did, Tracy's eyes filled with panic. They then led us to a private room with a television and a phone, and Tracy announced, "I don't like it."

The orderlies gently told Tracy what time meals would be and said different therapists would drop in and invited us to walk around the grounds. "You can leave at any time," I reminded him.

He stayed for a week.

The first time he attended group therapy, he didn't say a word about himself. "I tried to help the others," he told me later. "I don't have any problems compared to the problems the other people are talking about." After a few sessions, however, he opened up. Once I arrived just a bit early for a family therapy session and saw several people standing around Tracy, comforting him. He was wiping tears off his cheeks.

❦

At the end of a week, I took Tracy home. When we got settled inside, I made a confession.

The day after he'd told me he wanted to kill himself, the perfect day we'd spent together, I had hidden his pistols. Pills hadn't occurred to me, but the guns had, so I had hidden them.

I couldn't live like that, I confessed. That was living a life of distrust. I showed him where the guns were hidden and said, "You can put them back where you want, if you wish." It was my way of saying, here, I'm handing you back control of your life. It was also my way of saying, I trust you. Let's move on.

33

Taking a Stand

Tracy

Summer 1995

Over the summer, home alone, I had plenty of time to think about where I'd been and what I'd learned.

Depression, I now knew, was a sickness that required treatment. I took my medication faithfully and went to therapy regularly. Amtrak was gracious in granting me time to get better. I didn't go back to work until early August.

One night Judy and I were sitting in the Jacuzzi. She said, "You know, we've been through a unique experience. We should take a stand and talk about it."

"What do you mean? We are talking about it. We're talking about it right now. We talk about it all the time."

"No," she said. "We should tell everyone we can, hey, this needs changing. This system needs improving. It is a caterpillar that needs to be a butterfly. It needs to change so that no one else has to go through what you went through." She paused. "We've got to write a book."

"What?" I said. "You've got to be sniffing glue if you think I'm going public with what I did. I mean, we managed to get through it without anybody knowing it, but the media would have a field day with this. You can't really believe I would do that."

Judy was very quiet for a long time. Then she looked at me, locked into my eyes, and said, "You really don't have a choice. You owe it to everyone still there. You cannot walk away from this. You've never walked away from anything. You felt like you failed when you were dismissed. You felt like you let the families down, the judge down, the prosecution down, the defense down, the other jurors down, Mr. Simpson down. This is the thing you can do for them. Help make the system better. You must."

That is how this book came to be. Both Judy and I hope it will play some part in effecting change. We both think the American way still represents the best hope in the world for justice. We just think the system needs some improvement. It can be difficult, however, to know what needs changing when so much of the court system goes on behind closed doors. It is our hope that this book opens some of those doors. After all, sunlight is indeed the best disinfectant.

Aftermath

A suicide gesture is one thing. A suicide attempt, a genuine attempt at ending one's life, is quite another. It's only natural to wonder which described Tracy Kennedy's overdose.

"This was no gesture," said neurologist Bruce Weimer. "This was an attempt."

Echoed Raymond Manning, the psychiatrist who treated Tracy at Las Encinas Hospital, "He made a suicide attempt."

Before sequestration, Weimer said, Tracy "was a very normal, affable, outgoing person." Afterward, "he came in and I was literally shocked by the difference in his appearance. He was withdrawn and depressed. He was physically and mentally slow. If you didn't know him, the difference might not have been so striking. But having seen him in a normal state and having seen him in this state, there was obviously a major change in his personality. He was frank about this. He was really having difficulty coping emotionally and mentally with—as he put it—having let everybody down."

Stressing that he is not a psychiatrist, Weimer said he nonetheless will "occasionally gently suggest [to a patient] that maybe a problem is emotionally related, that perhaps a counselor would be a good idea. I'm not one to usually insist on psychiatric intervention. But in this situation I made an exception.

"I told him as bluntly and as matter-of-factly as possible. 'You need a psychiatrist.' I said, 'This is more than one person can handle. It's more than you can handle. You need psychiatric help.'

"He said, 'Well, I think I can shake it off.'" He wanted the chance to try that first. I had prescribed an antidepressant for him, Zoloft. We agreed that if there wasn't a fairly rapid improvement with the medication, he would then see a psychiatrist.

"Unfortunately, he apparently went home and overdosed on his wife's Xanax."

Xanax is not a "particularly lethal drug," Weimer said. But in large quantities—particularly the amount Tracy took—it could certainly have proven lethal.

He added, "It's only a miracle that [Judy Kennedy] didn't wake up the next morning to find him dead beside her. That apparently was what he had planned. This was not a hysterical call for help. This was a genuine suicide attempt."

What drove the attempt, according to Manning, was severe depression. Tracy had "all the major symptoms," including "profound" insomnia, loss of energy, loss of ability to concentrate, a "tremendously diminished" sense of self-esteem, and, "most importantly, a sense of hopelessness," he said.

"As is typically the case [with] severe depression, he felt he would not be able to function, felt he had let everyone down, and felt there was not much point in going on with his life," said Manning, associate director of Las Encinas's depressive disorders program.

Tracy's personality characteristics, Manning explained, made him particularly susceptible to depression: "He is a bit of a loner. His wife is his major companion in life. The impression I get is he certainly is not a gregarious social individual. He tends to be very perfectionistic, somewhat obsessive in his style."

Given those characteristics, Manning said, Tracy was "extremely vulnerable to exactly the stresses he faced" during sequestration, including "enforced socialization. A loss of autonomy. A focus from the [sheriff's] deputies: 'Accept authority and shut up.' "

In addition, Tracey felt "caught in a terrible bind," Manning said. He came to view sequestration "as really unfair and demeaning. But because of his own internal perfectionistic ways, he felt this obligation to be a good juror.

"The situation was eating him up," Manning

added. "To quit or cop out was really totally unacceptable in terms of his own conscience . . . but when he was let go, what was he to do? They found him wanting, they let him go. He let everybody down—that was his feeling. He was already severely depressed. And this was totally intolerable."

At Las Encinas, Manning reported, Tracy finally was willing to accept the notion that depression is an illness, a sickness having nothing to do with one's will or motivation. Once Tracy made that leap, Manning said, it made it much easier to get onto the road to recovery.

Both Manning and Weimer believe Tracy is already well along that road.

"He's much more like the person I knew before this whole thing," Weimer said.

ALAN ABRAHAMSON
August, 1995